MW01516915

In July 1998 I was sentenced to four months in prison for simple assault. I guess not many people in my home town of Squamish felt much sympathy for me. And to be honest, I didn't deserve any. I was only 19 but already I had a rap sheet as long as my leg. I'd been in and out of Youth Detention Centres for years, but now I was no longer classed as a juvenile. For as long as I could remember I'd been acting the man, and now the court considered me one. So instead of being sent to one of British Columbia's youth facilities I was taken to the Fraser Regional Correctional Centre in Abbotsford, British Columbia. A 'Correctional Centre' is what in the old days they called 'prison'.

It was my first time in an adult prison, and it was a hell of a shock compared to what I'd grown used to in the Youth Detention Centres. There you were out in the open for a lot of the time, doing forestry work; the guards were called 'supervisors', and the inmates were 'students'. Not in Matsqui. We were 'cons', and most of the day was spent in our cells.

What made those first few days worse was the knowledge that I had another assault charge to answer. The four month sentence had come with 18 months suspended, so I knew there was a good chance that my stay at Fraser Regional would be more than just a few weeks.

That's what happened. At the end of October I was back in court, this time charged with two counts of assaults for a fight I'd been involved with the previous November. I was held on remand, returned to Fraser Regional while the legal wheels of my case began to turn. Slowly.

Looking back on my time in prison it's hard to recall what it was like. That's because each day was the same. Groundhog Day. I remember that we'd be out of our cells at 8 in the morning. Breakfast was followed by school for some inmates, manual work for others. I did school. It passed the time. So did working out. That became the highlight of each day. Pumping iron in the prison gym, doing push ups and sit ups in my cell. In the evenings we'd play a bit of sport in the yard. It helped burn off the boredom, and it kept me out of trouble inside

In the spring of 1999 I was released. When I stepped outside I was met by my mum. I'd put my parents through the ringer over the years. They'd done everything in their power to steer me in the right direction but the change had to come from me. I could either carry on being a prick, and look forward to return trips to Fraser Regional, or I could sort my shit out.

In prison I'd mixed with a lot of different people. There were opportunities for me in Vancouver, criminal opportunities, and the toughest challenge for any newly-released offender is what to do and where to go in the first first days of freedom. If there is no strong support network in place it's easy to slip back into the bad old ways. But I'd had plenty of time to think inside. That's one of the few benefits of being locked up in a cell on your own.

Every day I'd considered my future. I'd been a jackass at school and had few qualifications to boast. And who'd want to employ some punk who had spent most of his teens in and out of correctional centres? In prison you need to have a goal on which to focus, something outside that gives you hope as you waste away days in your cell. I had that something - rugby.

I was good at it, I enjoyed it and most importantly, rugby gave me an outlet to be physical without getting in trouble with the law.

When mum collected me from prison she had my rugby boots in the back of the car. We drove straight to Trout Lake Park, in East Vancouver, where the Squamish Axemen Rugby Club were playing a game.

I walked out of prison and into the dressing room. There was a bit of banter as I got changed, a few wisecracks, but none of the boys passed judgement. I ran out onto the pitch and breathed a sigh of relief. Freedom. Looking back nearly 20 years that was the defining moment of my life. I had a choice when I came out of prison: go straight or go back to jail. Rugby helped me make the right choice.

[ends]

Chapter One

My paternal grandfather died in 1992, around the time I embarked on my adolescent life of crime. It was probably just as well he wasn't alive to see all the trouble I caused - as an ex-policeman he might not have approved. He was from London, and joined the Metropolitan Police in the late 1930s. When the Second World War broke out he enlisted in the Royal Air Force and served as a flight engineer in a Lancaster bomber. I've spoken to my dad about my grandfather and he remembers him as a big, strong man - about 1,88m - who was quiet and compassionate. He must have been affected by what he went through during the war but he didn't tell my dad much about his experiences. It meant a huge amount to him, however, that was clear with the request in his will: that his ashes be scattered from a Lancaster bomber over the English Channel. My dad and my uncle wrote to the RAF, not that confident the request would be granted. But it was. My dad brought me over the service and to say I was proud as I watched the Lancaster fly overhead would be an understatement.

My grandfather didn't play rugby, his team sport was the tug-of-war, which was a big thing in the British police back then. My grandfather was the anchor, the guy at the back with the biggest muscles.

After the war my grandparents moved from London to Littlehampton, on the Sussex coast. My dad was born in 1949 and one of his earliest memories is of my grandfather pedalling his police bike around the streets of Littlehampton.

Dad went to school in Chichester, along the coast from Littlehampton, and it was there that the Cudmore family was introduced to rugby. He was coached at school, by Roger Quittenton, who later became a referee and officiated at the inaugural World Cup in 1987. Dad developed into a pretty handy player. He had a similar physique to his dad, and represented Sussex Schools in the back-row before going to Cambridge University to read Medical Science.

He was on course to win a University Blue in his second year - playing in a XV that included Keith Hughes, who won a handful of caps for Wales - but shortly before the Varsity Match he tore his ankle ligaments and that was his chance gone.

After Cambridge my dad moved to London to continue his studies at the Westminster Medical School. From what I gather he burned a lot of midnight oil in the capital. There were his clinical training, his rugby - he was a member of the Westminster XV that won the Hospitals Cup for the first time in 1974 - and then there were the parties. At one dance he met the woman who would become his wife, and my mum.

How to best describe my mum? Part bohemian, part nomad, she's certainly a unique lady with an award from the Royal Lifesaving Society for rescuing two drowning children. She grew up in London, not too far from Twickenham stadium, and her dad was an oil economist for Esso. As a kid mum was passionate about ballet, art and travelling - and she still is. Her dream was to become a ballet dancer but she grew too tall

Mum came of age during London's Swinging Sixties and she had a blast, by all accounts. Her parents were consumed by their work so she had an unusual amount of freedom for a teenager. She used it well, or so she tells me! The music scene at this time in London was awesome and mum saw the Rolling Stones, Eric Clapton,

Elton John and the Moody Blues all live. Not in the huge venues they play today, but in the pubs and clubs of London. In some ways mum lived the stereotypical life of the young woman during the late 1960s. She was into the growing women's liberation movement and she was a bit of a hippy, travelling with friends in a VW bus around Europe, and generally seeking out fresh adventures and new challenges wherever she could find them.

Eventually she decided it was time to get a profession. She enrolled at nursing school but left after about a year and a half when she realised it wasn't the job for her. She needed something more creative, and for a while worked for various advertising agencies in London before landing a job

managing Promotions for all artists on WEA Records labels. But she'd kept in touch with some of her nursing friends and at one of their medical parties she met my dad. They married in 1973 and while dad finished his medical studies at the Royal College of Physicians, mum completed a degree in Education and Psychology at the University of London.

By the time they'd qualified they were both wanting to leave the UK. Mum, because she wanted to travel and seek out new adventures, and dad because he felt morale in the British National Health Service was at rock bottom. This was a time when Britain was called the 'Sick Man of Europe' and so mum and dad decided to leave before they became infected.

An opportunity arose for dad to head out to Canada for six weeks and work in a rural medical practice in Saskatchewan. So he took it, and he loved it. Apparently when he arrived the English doctor he was replacing was revving his car in the driveway he was so desperate to get the hell out! But mum and dad threw themselves into the work and embraced the new culture and community, and when the six weeks were up they were sorry to leave. Returning to London made them realise how much they missed Canada. There was only one remedy - emigrate. This was 1977 and already the entry requirements were being tightened so you were awarded more points on your visa if you applied for work in a remote area. That wasn't a problem for mum and dad. So in March 1978 they packed their bags and headed to Teulon, Manitoba, a town of about 1,000 inhabitants 40 miles north of Winnipeg. It was minus 27 when they arrived. Welcome to Canada.

Luckily summer soon arrived, and a short while later so did I. I entered the world on September 6, 1978 weighing in at 9lbs 3oz. Dad, who knows a thing or two about babies, having delivered hundreds over the years, tells me I was a "strange baby who was very dense". Thanks dad! I think he means 'dense' as in heavy. Apparently people used to grunt with the effort of picking me up.

I was born in Winnipeg but in another sign of how intrepid my mum and dad were, we left Teulon a month after I was born and relocated to British Columbia.

Mum and dad packed all their worldly goods into a Volkswagen Rabbit - I was in a basket on the back seat - and hit the road, driving 1,500 miles until they reached the town of Squamish. In the late 1970s Squamish was a real redneck town, one of the logging centres of Canada with a reputation for hard-living and hard-working. But it was only 50 miles north of Vancouver and the six months in Teulon had taught mum and dad that though they loved Canada, they didn't want to be super-remote. Squamish was within easy reach of the ski slopes of Whistler while Vancouver had restaurants, theatres and museums. Everyone was happy.

It's taken just a few paragraphs to describe how I ended up to be the first Canadian to emerge from a lineage of Brits and it feels like I've done my parents a disservice. I have nothing but respect and admiration for the decisions they took nearly 40 years ago, decisions that required courage, daring and initiative. I've sometimes wondered what might have happened if they'd been more conservative and less willing to take risks. I'd be English for one thing.

One story that my dad likes to tell encapsulates the new life on which he'd embarked. On the Saturday after he and mum had arrived in Squamish there was a Sportsmen's Dinner at the local Rotary Club. Dad was invited - it was a men-only affair - and off he went not quite sure what to expect. He'd been to a lot of sports' dinners during his years of medical studies but they'd been typically English. Everyone wearing black tie and drinking sherry. The Squamish Sportsmen's Dinner was a little different. Within half an hour two people had slid from their chairs dead drunk, and dad had to then munch his way through the local wildlife, from salmon to beaver and even chewing a couple of moose balls. The highlight of the evening was a raffle and one of the prizes on offer was a nice, new shiny axe. Guess who had the winning ticket? To roars of laugher, the new town doctor was presented with a axe.

Chapter Two

I was a challenge for my parents from just about day one. When I asked mum and dad what I was like as a baby the first thing they both said was 'you didn't sleep much'. I was colicky, too, and if I wasn't crying in those first few months I was always on the move. This got worse as the months progressed. I would never sit still and wanted to explore everything. Apparently it didn't take me long to master the child locks and with our house conquered I moved further afield. One of my mum's earliest memories is of me wandering off down the street dressed in my diaper and wearing rubber boots and a t-shirt.

As I grew from a toddler into a child my size began to become an issue. I was so much bigger and stronger that the other kids that I sometimes hurt them unintentionally. In gymnastics classes I to go on the trampoline by myself otherwise the moment I took my first bounce all the other kids went flying.

From a very young age my parents introduced me to the Great Outdoors. There are photos in the family albums of me as a baby in a back sack, being taken for hikes around the local lakes or up mountains by mum and dad. Not only did they love nature but they also shared the same view about bringing up kids - don't overprotect. They gave me and my brothers, Luke and Daniel, as much physical freedom as possible, and I don't ever remember being told off for coming home dirty or blooded. And that happened frequently. But having a doctor as a dad meant that it was only the serious scrapes that meant a trip to the Western medical clinic; most of the time dad stitched us up on the kitchen table. He's got a typically matter-of-fact bedside manner: 'Don't worry, son, this won't hurt'. Meanwhile there's me screaming and crying because it really does hurts like hell.

Dad says that from an early age it was obvious I was a risk-taker. People either are, or they aren't, and I definitely was. My environment gave me the freedom to take risks, so I took them, and when I look back on my childhood the word that best sums it up is 'wonderful'.

Our house was in the Garibaldi highlands on the north-east side of town. It was beautiful passive solar home on an acre of property. Dad had built it and we had majestic views over the mountains and water. The back door opened onto a huge expanse of forest and that was where we raced around on our bikes or fought our wars with sticks as guns. In the summer we'd be tubing down the rivers or camping out around log fires, and in the winter we'd head up into the mountains, snowmobiling in Brohm Ridge or skiing in Whistler. Dad also had a boat that we used to explore the Pacific North west, visiting all the islands that lay between Vancouver Island and the mainland.

Then there were the more unusual sports, like raccoon wars. Me and my buddies would chase after them with baseball bats but, man, those little bastards are tough to kill! Snagging salmon was easier, particularly when they were spawning. It wasn't very legal but when you're eight or nine, you don't really worry about things like that. We'd put four or five barbed hooks on a line and zing the line across the river. Then we pulled it in as fast as we could and sometimes there would be two or three fish on the line. We didn't take the fish home for supper - that would have been far too sensible. We were young boys so we used the fish as baseball bats, swinging wildly at each other and squirting eggs all over the place to gross each other out. Yeah, it's not too politically correct, but growing up in the British Columbia wilderness wasn't a place for the faint-hearted. You had to be tough to survive. I remember one night we were upstairs when we heard the garbage cans hit the ground outside. Dad came down to investigate, opened the back door and there was a huge black bear looking for any leftovers. Dad didn't introduce himself. Slamming shut the door he ran upstairs and we spent the next half an hour watching the bear from the deck. Once he'd been through the garbage he sauntered back to the forest. Looking back on those childhood years I can see what an influence they had on my later life. I've mentioned learning about risks, but also learning how to adapt, how to cope and how to make the best of a bad job. One of the biggest things about being a Canadian is we don't make too much noise about anything. I learned that as a child, ironically from my English parents, although they're both of a generation who grew up in the austerity of post-war Britain when you learned to make do with what little you had.

The other major influence in my childhood was the Squamish Nation, a very powerful native band who are descended from the Coast Salish Aboriginal peoples who lived in the west coast of Canada. In recent years Squamish has changed beyond all recognition. The logging industry has declined, the saw mills have gone, and it's been gentrified, a bedroom community for Vancouver and Whistler. Tell people now that you have a house in Squamish and people shoot you jealous looks; when I was a kid people from Vancouver regarded as us rednecks.

The 'rednecks' was the name given to the loggers - most of whom were of European descent - but there were two other ethnic groups in Squamish. They were a fair few Indians, who'd emigrated from East India to work in the paper mills, and of course there were the Squamish Natives. I found myself between the Natives and the Rednecks, trying to avoid the confrontations that frequently erupted between the three groups.

I've always had a huge respect for the Squamish Nation. My first school was Totem Hall nursery , on the Stawamus Reserve, and it was just about the only time I enjoyed education. I learned about the Native culture, their history, their language, and also more practical things such as building wigwams and identifying wild flowers and fauna. Much later, in my teenage years, I had a spell playing lacrosse for the North Shore Indians, alongside some of my Native buddies I'd known since primary school. I was about the only redneck in the team and my job as a defenceman was to stop any attack coming through. I did that by fair means or foul. I was, in lacrosse parlance, a Goon.

In the 1997 season we won the British Columbia Lacrosse Association Provincial Championships, which still ranks as one of my proudest sporting achievements. We had a great team and playing matches on the Reservation was special. The place would be packed and the atmosphere unbelievable.

They're a fine people, the Squamish Nation, a warrior race and in terms of athletic ability they are outstanding. I played rugby with quite a few of them and they are hard hitters. They're also a fiercely loyal and honourable people, and I'll never forget the support they offered me when I hit rock bottom in my teenage years. Whenever I'm back in Squamish I'll visit my old buddies on the Reservation and the years drop away and it's like nothing has changed. Most of them have satellite TV now, so they've been able to watch quite of few my matches. When I first moved to France they didn't really understand how I could make a living from playing rugby. They assumed club rugby in France was like club rugby in Canada, watched by a few hundred people. They're all huge hockey fans and so the first time they saw me playing for Clermont at the Stade Marcel-Michelin they understood. Rugby in France is what the NHL is in Canada.

I've always felt comfortable among the Squamish Nation. They're a good, honest, uncomplicated people, as were most of the 'redneck' families I knew growing up. My family background is middle-class but I've always preferred the company of working men to businessmen. That's part of my character but it's also a great deal to do with my mum and dad. They taught me never to treat anyone differently just because of their class. That's another reason why I'm delighted I was born a Canadian. The English class system is something I don't understand, considering yourself better than someone just because you have more money or a bigger house.

You earn respect through your actions, not because of what school you went to or what your dad does for a living.

One way to earn respect in Squamish among my peers was through sport. My first love was football and 'Soccer Saturday' was my favourite TV programme. It was a highlights show of all the action from the English Premier League, or First Division as it was in the late 1980s. Me and my buddies were hooked on that, and as soon as the show ended we would go outside and kick a ball around. I played centre-forward and I wasn't too bad, at least not in the early years. But as I got older and bigger I kept getting booked every time I made a tackle. Me and referees have never really seen eye to eye.

My other sport was skiing. I started when I was about two and a half and by the time I was nine I was skiing for Blackcomb, which is a club in Whistler. That was awesome at first. Each weekend we'd go off to a different mountain and dream of being the next Mike Carney. Mike was a Squamish boy who had skied for Canada in the 1988 Calgary Olympics. His old man was a good buddy of my dad's, and occasionally Mike would come round to our house. When he did I was completely star struck.

Downhill skiing was my thing. It was the most dangerous, the most glamorous and the fastest. I had some pretty spectacular crashes - concussion, a few broken bones - but that wasn't what eventually made me fall out of love with competitive skiing. It was the coaching. Four or five days a week just doing gates, gates, gates. It became boring and by my mid-teens I was burned out.

Also, I saw what my buddies were up to it and that looked more fun - snowmobiling. It had the adrenaline of skiing but more importantly for a teenage kid, it had camaraderie. Brohm Ridge was our favourite spot. There was a local cabin where we'd meet and then we'd spent the day dropping cornices and highmarking in our snowmobiles. Dropping cornices is pretty straightforward, it's just launching the mobile off a cornice, but highmarking has its risks. You head up the mountain in your mobile - most of ours were 5 or 600cc - and then your turn round and come back down without losing power. One danger is rolling the snowmobile but the biggest risk is triggering an avalanche. A lot of it is about common sense, being familiar with the terrain and assessing the avalanche risk, so we never triggered any. I was once caught in an avalanche, skiing in the Blackhorn Mountains, and it's not an experience I'd like to repeat.

I went off a cornice and as soon as I landed I heard the 'crack' of the snow. Frightening. I winged it but I had no chance against nature. The avalanche caught me very quickly and took my legs. Down I went, and all I could do was start swimming. I managed to keep my top half above the snow but in those few eerie seconds when the snow comes to a rest it felt like I was encased in concrete. Fortunately I had a buddy with me, who had been clear of the avalanche's path, and with his help I was able to dig myself out.

But some of my friends weren't so lucky. Of the kids I grew up with in Squamish, three died young, including one of my closest buddies. We lost Ryan Taylor in 1996 when he was 17. He and Phil Lacoursiere were killed when their car collided head-on with a pick-up truck. The following year Chris Heidenreich and Paul Hopkins were on Brohm Ridge when their snowmobile hit something and went out of control. They plunged off a 30 metre cliff and Chris was killed on impact. Paul survived, somehow, despite the fact he was trapped under snowmobile for the night with terrible injuries in freezing temperatures.

Then in 2002 came the death that hit me hardest. I'd just won my first cap for Canada and signed my first professional contract, with Llanelli Scarlets, and life was going well. So it was, too, for Josh Chapman. He and I went back a long way and he was a rising star in Canadian extreme sports. He was an international snowboarder with a sponsorship deal and the press were beginning to feature him in articles. He was getting a reputation for pushing the limits, even in the world of extreme sports, and it was to push that reputation to the maximum that he dreamed up this stunt of riding a snowmobile through a wall of flame in Squamish Business Park. There was a film crew on hand, and quite a crowd, but no safety precautions were in place. From what I understand bales of hay were doused in petrol and ignited but as Josh drove through the wall of fire someone threw a bucket of gasoline. Josh was engulfed by flames and suffered burns to 85% of his body. He died two weeks later.

Chapter Three

I was twelve when I first broke the law. I'd had an argument with my mum and took the family car for a joy ride. I drove straight past a police car and looked at the officer. He looked at me and I knew straight away what he was thinking - "I don't think he's old enough to be driving". I zipped up the road back home but the police car followed and minutes after getting into the house there was a knock on the door. Dad was at work at the time but mum, who was already very upset because I'd damaged the car, answered the door. My dad got involved and told the policeman to deal with me harshly, which they the Royal Canadian Mounted Police did. I was taken to the station, and ended up with 100 hours of community service and a one-year probation.

It was around this time that mum and dad got divorced. There were no signs of problems in their marriage but my dad is old school English, a reserved gentleman, doesn't raise his voice much. I never saw any big arguments between them so it was a surprise when they announced they were splitting. But they handled it in a pretty dignified manner. I was pleased because mum went to live in Whistler so that meant more opportunities to hang out on the skip slopes with my buddies.

Of course, I've asked myself if my behaviour was linked to my parents' separation. But, honestly, I don't think it was. I remember that excuse was used during one of my many court appearances; my defence lawyer told the court that "his parents have recently divorced and this has had a great affect on him". I was listening to him in the dock, thinking "No, that's not it all, buddy, I just want to have fun".

To be honest I was a little prick from way before my parents split. I would run around the whole time, just acting crazy. There was one time, when I was about five, when we went on a family holiday to Hawaii and I was practically unmanageable on the plane.

So that wild streak was always there and unfortunately as I reached adolescence it grew from mischievousness into something more sinister. And yet I didn't go out looking for trouble. It's hard to explain: I just always wanted to do something fun and cool and fast. Make a noise. Even today that feeling hasn't completely vanished. Now and again I get an itch to go and something crazy but having a family, being a professional athlete, keeps it in check. But twenty years ago I didn't know the meaning of the word 'responsibility'. Every day I looked for something extreme to do: skiing the steepest mountain, jumping off the biggest cliff into the river, and, yeah, fronting up to the toughest kids.

I began getting into a lot of fights: fights with people I knew, fights with people I didn't know and fights with people I might bump into at the gas station. It didn't take much for the first punch to be thrown. Any perceived slight would do it, a lack of respect. Writing these words now, it sounds pretty pathetic, but when you're a teenager with a small-town mentality you don't allow yourself to be disrespected in your own territory And I was unable to walk away. The opposite. It would come to blows really fast. My strategy was 'you've got to go from zero to 100 faster than the other guy, because otherwise you're going to lose the fight'. So I hit first and asked questions later.

I suffered a lot from growing pains between the ages of 12 and 14 - to the point where I stopped playing most sports because I had so much trouble with my knees. Even sitting in a car for thirty minutes was agony. Perhaps this created a frustration within me, the fact I had all this energy and I couldn't release it on the athletics track, the ski slopes or on the soccer field.

Perhaps this need to be respected was also something to do with the fact I was desperate to prove myself. I was a Squamish boy but my parents were English and middle-class, and my dad was the town doctor. But I'm making these judgements with twenty five years' hindsight. When you're a snotty-nosed kid you tend not to analyse your behaviour with too much depth.

The bottom line is I was a jackass with a growing reputation for trouble, and I have only myself to blame. Alcohol played its part in some of the fights but I was more into marijuana as a teenager. I smoked a shit load of weed, everybody did. It wasn't a question of 'doing drugs', it was just normal on the west coast of Canada. You'd spend the day snowboarding in the winter or down by the river in the summer, climbing rocks, having a good time, and you'd end the day smoking a joint.

Weed was as far as my drug-taking went. I never did anything stronger. Nor was I an "enforcer" for a drugs gang. There have been some lurid stories in the press over the years implying I went around British Columbia collecting the debts of drug gangs. No, it wasn't like that.

We smoked weed, one or two of my buddies sold it, and on the odd occasion when a buyer didn't pay up I'd go and ask for the cash. It was nothing organised, no big crime syndicate, but there were people I knew whose dads were involved in some pretty heavy stuff - supplying cocaine to the whole valley. There were definitely opportunities for me to go big-time into the drug-supplying scene, particularly with local biker gangs, but I'd seen a couple of friends go down that route and it was bad news. I might have been a prick, but I wasn't completely stupid.

Then again, my old school teachers might disagree with that last sentiment. Me and school never got on. I enjoyed the Totem Hall Native school but once in Brackendale junior high I ran riot. I didn't find it much if a challenge. The curriculum was quite easy, and I always find it hard to stay engaged the moment I understand something. On the other hand, if there was something that I didn't understand I wasn't interested because I considered myself to cool to sit and learn.

So the moment I began to get bored I played the class clown, fooling around, trying to be the cool legend who does crazy things at the weekend and then makes his own rules in class. The school didn't tolerate my 'craziness' for long. I was removed from Brackendale and sent to Howe Sound Secondary School and enrolled in their Reconnect Alternative Programme

Here I encountered Steve Lloyd. He was a great teacher, patient and kind, someone who dedicated his whole life to teaching kids with various difficulties. He also loved his rugby and encouraged me to take up the sport.

Steve sat in the middle of this open-plan classroom and our desks were all around him. On the first day he told us: "Listen, if you guys want to go off for a break, go ahead, but you've got to do your work". There was a sort of give-and-take philosophy, and I liked that. For the first time I knuckled down to school work, particularly history and geography, but while Mr Lloyd was straightening me out in the classroom, outside I was beginning to go off the rails.

My first experience of a youth detention centre was when I was sent to the Maples Adolescent Treatment Program in Burnaby, just east of Vancouver, for a series of assessments. The program dealt with kids who had behaviour issues and I definitely fell into that category. They wanted to know why I was a prick - though they couched it in more politically correct language! I was interviewed by some psychologists and attended various group therapy sessions as they tried to figure out why I was like I was. I didn't know what to say, other than I wanted to have fun. The 'fun' continued until the day a court tired of my behaviour and ordered my detention at Camp Trapping after I was found guilty of assault in December 1993. I was 15, and about to discover I wasn't quite so tough as I thought.

Camp Trapping is in Prince George. Prince George is in the middle of nowhere. To be exact, it's 450 miles north of Squamish. It wasn't a youth detention centre as such, it was more of a Wilderness Camp. We weren't locked up in cells but you didn't escape from Camp Trapping , at least not unless you fancied hiking through hundreds of miles of bush. It was a very remote camp, and though I didn't know it at the time Camp Trapping taught me much about life.

The camp's motto was "I Think I Can, Therefore I Can". There were no guards, there were 'counsellors' and the inmates - there were only 14 - were called 'students'. But don't go thinking this was some touchy-feely camp. Much of its approach was based along military lines. There was no running water at the camp so on arrival we were shown to a sauna and told to work up a sweat and soap ourselves down. This struck me as quite cool. Then the sauna door opened and we were ordered out and told to jump in the lake. This was December, in northern Canada. It was freezing. We went down to the lake. It was covered by a film of ice. We can't jump in, we protested. Break the ice and jump, we were told. Damn, it was cold, and we had to do that every day for four months.

Each day started at six. We were out of our bunks and making our beds, not just making them but crafting the four corners with army precision. Then we went on a run. It was normally 16km but every two months we did a 50k run. That was fun. Some mornings it was so cold we ran with a sock over our cock because we were worried it would freeze and drop off. If the thermometer dipped below about minus 20 we would spared the morning run and instead do an hour's callisthenics, what we call cross-training today.

There was a points system at Camp Trapping, and if I remember rightly you had points deducted if you didn't do your chores well, and if you were caught swearing. The purpose was to do each chore to the maximum, and so it became important to a bunch of undisciplined kids to to be precise in everything we did. In that way we had the most points possible at the end of the week, and with the points came little privileges, such as being able to take an extra book from the library.

There was no electricity at Camp Trapping so our heat came from firewood. But with no power tools we students were obliged to gather it the old-fashioned way. So each morning off we went into the forest with these big saws to in search of fallen trees. We'd then chop them up, drag the big chunks back through the snow, before splitting them into smaller pieces at the camp. The whole process made you realise too how tough life was a century ago for our forebears, and how easy it is today in comparison. But there was a sense of satisfaction at the end of the day in having done our tasks well and having 'survived' another day in the wilderness through our own endeavours.

It was hard and monotonous work, but looking back there's no doubt that those four months in Camp Trapping had a profound effect on me. I'd spent weeks chopping down trees yet something had taken root inside me. I'd seen the rewards that discipline, perseverance and precision could bring, and though it would require a few more years, those roots would help me grow into a decent human being.

Chapter Four

When I returned to Squamish from Camp Trapping I stayed out of trouble for nearly a year. I didn't fancy going back to the wilderness and I tried to knuckle down at school. But it's hard not to slip back into your bad old ways, however hard you try not to. In October 1994 I spent three weeks at Burnaby Youth Open Custody Centre for curfew violations, and in early 1995 I got into another fight and was convicted of assault. It wasn't a serious scrap but set alongside my curfew violations of the previous autumn the court came down on me heavily.

I was despatched to the Boulder Bay Youth Custody Centre where I remained until August 1996. This place was close to Maple Ridge, about 100 kilometres south of Squamish, and it was every bit as remote as Camp Trapping. Boulder Bay (which closed down in 2002) was constructed on the narrow forested area between upper and lower Alouette Lake. It was a hell of slog to reach the Boulder Bay, which was built from the remains of an old gold prospectors camp nearby. The only way to reach the camp was a half-hour boat trip and then a half mile hike through the forest. Similarly supplies could only be brought in by boat and it was one of the inmates' tasks to wheelbarrow the provisions from the shore to the camp. Like Camp Trapping, Boulder Bay only held a small number of offenders - 36 in total, split into three groups of twelve who lived in huts along with one or two supervisors. Boulder Bay had been established in the late 1960s to instil in youth offenders work, survival and leadership skills, based on the Outward Bound instruction given to Canadian sailor during the Second World War. There was a particular emphasis on

teamwork, working together to complete the tasks, which lasted from 8 in the morning until 4.45 in the afternoon. We then had an hour for supper and from 5.45 to 9 we had course work that included map navigation, first aid, canoeing and ropes and knots. Sunday was one the day of rest, of sorts. We had a four hour hike from 11 to 3 and in the evening our weekly treat was a movie. It was a hard life but again, as schooling for life, the 18 months I spent at Boulder Bay were far more practical than any high school.

I left Boulder Bay a month shy of my 18th birthday. I was on the cusp of adulthood and yet I had little to show for it in terms of academic qualifications. I'd completed such school certificates at Boulder Bay but the prospect of returning to education didn't appeal to me. Seeing all the letters after my old man's name, that was impressive, but it was also alien, the whole idea of studying to achieve that. My experiences at Camps Trapping and Wilderness had shown that I liked working outdoors and using my hands. The obvious answer was to became a logger. I got some work for a local company and was soon earning about 20 bucks an hour - not bad for an ex-con!

I was boxing in my spare time, too, and doing some wrestling and power-lifting, so I was a big old boy for my age. Unfortunately I hadn't matured emotionally. **I continued to get in fights and by now I realised my size was intimidating for a lot of people. And, yeah, I got a kick out of that.**

Part of me felt I was invincible and I'm ashamed to say now that I enjoyed my growing reputation as a hard man. In everything I've ever done I've always pushed myself to be the best I, and that included being the hardest kid in Squamish. I kept out of trouble most of the time but in March 1997 I was back in court, and once more the charge was assault. It was another fight with kids from out of town and my punishment was two weeks in Burnaby youth detention centre.

What I never stopped to consider was the effect my behaviour was having on my parents. I caused them a lot of stress because of the stupid shit I was doing and yet they were doing everything in their power to try and stop me ruining my life. But my life was starting to spiral out of control and the events of December 31 1997

devastated my parents but more significantly they shattered the world of the McIntosh family.

The party I threw on New Year's Eve 1997 has become infamous. Not just in Squamish but in Vancouver and the whole of British Columbia. There's been a book written about it, a feature film, a documentary and thousands of newspaper articles devoted to what exactly happened. A lot of what's been written is plain wrong, just wild media exaggeration. Depending on which newspaper you picked up, there were between 100 and 200 people at the party. Everyone was dead drunk, doing drugs, it was a wild orgy. Just inaccurate shit. Here's what happened.

In November 1997 my dad remarried, to a lovely woman called Lois. I had no problem with his remarrying. On the morning of the wedding I played rugby, then I changed into my tuxedo and sank a couple of beers with the boys before heading to the church. Dad and Lois then went off to Mexico over Christmas on a belated honeymoon leaving me at home. My two brothers, Daniel and Luke, were living with mum.

Before he left on honeymoon dad asked mum to keep an eye on the house. He'd told me 'no parties' and mum said she would swing by from time to time to make sure I was behaving myself. It's been said and written that dad had asked Bob McIntosh to watch over the house in his absence. This is not true.

I'm ashamed to say I went behind dad's back and threw a party on New Year's Eve. It was supposed to be a fairly low-key party but more people arrived than I'd invited. Nonetheless even at its height there were no more than fifty people in the house.

About midway during the evening - before midnight - I popped down the road to the local Legion where the rugby club was having a New Year's Eve fund-raising event. I'd started playing regularly for the Squamish Axemen and I wanted to show my face. Before leaving I sought out my two buddies, Ryan McMillan and Ryan Howie, and told them to look after the house for the short time I was gone. Howie was downstairs and McMillan was upstairs, on the mezzanine between the ground floor and the first floor, chilling with his girlfriend. I knew Ryan McMillan well. We went way back and he was my size and had a hell of a right hook. I asked him to stop anyone going into my dad's room. I knew I could trust him and by **this time me and my buddies had a bit of an aura about us.**

But, anyway, there was an unwritten rule among us: if you had a house party your friends didn't disrespect your parents' property. Sure, a beer might be spilt, there'd be some weed smoked, but no hurling chairs through windows or puking up on the carpets.

I had no worries about leaving the party to go to the legion. The music was loud, people were having fun, but no one was out of control and the two Ryans were in charge.

It was a good house to have a party because of its location. We had no immediate next door neighbours. Bob and Katy McIntosh, and their four-year-old twins, were our nearest neighbours but their house was up a hill and aong a narrow track. My dad was not only the family doctor of the McIntoshes, he was also their friend. They'd been to his recent wedding and Bob, like my dad, was a keen triathlete. Sometimes they'd train together.

Bob was 40, a hell of a nice guy, and a dynamic one, too. When he thought the music was getting a little too loud he called the house to check everything was OK. Whoever answered the phone couldn't find me, so Bob tried again a few minutes later. Same response.

So he left the dinner party he was hosting and with a couple of friends, came to investigate. When they couldn't find me Bob began to take control. And that's how the clash happened. My buddies were big guys who carried themselves as adults, and when another adult appeared telling them what to do, telling them they needed to listen to what he was saying, they weren't going to take it. Bob left his friends downstairs and headed upstairs, where he ran into Ryan McMillan. Bob, being a lawyer, was strong-handed and he expected a young person to do as he said. But Ryan was like,'fuck you, beat it, Jamie told me to watch this floor'. Words were exchanged and then Ryan dropped Bob with one of his right hooks. For Ryan, that was it. Fight over, point made.

I was back from the legion within the hour. There were cars all over the driveway so

I had to park some way from the house and then walk up to the house. That's when I heard the sirens. There were no cellphones in those days - or least, we didn't have any - so the first I knew about what had happened was when I stepped through the front door. I saw Ryan McMillan and asked what was going on. He seemed bewildered, and mumbled something about hitting a guy, who'd gone down. Who did you hit? I asked. He wasn't sure.

When the ambulance left with Bob the cops stayed and turned the house into a crime scene. They took witness statements but because the fight had happened upstairs few people had much to say because most guests were downstairs. I wasn't too concerned at this point. There was no great pools of blood anywhere and if it was just a punch like Ryan had said a young, fit guy like Bob would be OK.

A few hours later I got a call at home from Greg Richmond, the player- president of the Squamish Axemen, who told me Bob had died. I couldn't believe it. I was in shock. Greg didn't know any further details so I went up to the hospital to try and figure out what had happened. But no one would tell me anything other than Bob was dead. I came back to the house and desperately tried to get hold of my dad but it wasn't until the next day that I finally spoke to him. I'll never forget that conversation. Dad was completely distraught. His friend had been killed, in his house, in a party thrown by his son behind his back.

It put an amazing amount of stress on him and the relationship with his new wife. Understandably she didn't want to live in a house that someone had died in and they moved out. For 18 months the house that my dad had built with his own hands was rented, and then eventually sold.

As for the relationship with my dad, it was severely tested. He'd just about reached the end of his tether, He didn't know what to do with me. He kept asking 'how could you let this happen?', and all I could say was 'I don't know'.

It would be five years before the truth emerged of what actually that night. In the interim a wall of silence was erected in Squamish among the people present when Bob was killed. I tried to break through the wall, asking everyone who'd been in the party what had happened, but most people had been downstairs. Of course I asked

Ryan McMillan but he just said "I hit the guy and then went downstairs". He was arrested and charged with manslaughter but in September 1998 the charges were stayed because of inconsistencies in the witness statements. It took the police five years to finally bring the killer to justice. During an undercover operation, Ryan Aldridge admitted to a detective that after Bob had been knocked out by McMillan, he had kicked him several times in the head. One of the blows caused an arterial tear that resulted in a brain haemorrhage. I knew Aldridge. He wasn't really a buddy of mine but we'd hung out together over the years. In December 2002 he was sentenced to five years in prison after admitting a charge of manslaughter.

McMillan pleaded guilty to assault and received a three-year suspended sentence. In an act of incredible compassion, Katy, Bob's widow, visited Ryan in prison and forgave him for killing her husband and the father of her two children. In the years following his release, Ryan and Katy haven a series of lectures on rehabilitation and forgiveness.

When a film was made of the killing in 2010 it was called 'Bond of Silence'. I haven't seen it but I imagine it doesn't reflect well on me or my friends. Why should it? As to why no one went to the police, there is no justification. We were young and immature, and we'd grown up with a belief that we should always keep our mouths shut. That made things worse because it seemed to the outside world that the killer was bring protected by Squamish.

Katy and I have never spoken since Bob's death. I should have gone and said sorry but I didn't know what to say. So I just left it. In the book she subsequently wrote, she said I had a "notorious" reputation and my "behaviour was often a topic of discussion in our house". I've no doubt it was. In the weeks after Bob's death I came in for a lot of press attention. My past misdemeanours were pored over in the media and there were reporters and camera crews camped at the bottom of the driveway. Fortunately they left my dad and brothers alone; it was me they were after but I didn't give them a minute of my time.

A few months after Bob's death Katy launched a civil suit against me and my dad. I thought that was beyond cheap to drag my dad into it. He'd been in Mexico, he'd told me 'no parties', and yet Katy wanted to sue him for negligence for failing to protect Bob's safety. The bottom line is that Bob had no business being at the party. He wasn't invited. He just came barnstorming into the house expecting everyone to bow down to him. He was unfortunately in over his head. Yes, he was faced with people younger than him, but he didn't understand that the group of guys were looking after my house and my interests. He took the brunt of them trying to protect my house It was miscommunication, misunderstanding, that erupted into terrible violence. It was a horrible situation but I was angry with Katy for trying to get monetary gain out of the death of her husband. She's denied that was ever the intention but whatever her motivation, early in 2000 she dropped the suit. Nonetheless her decision to launch the suit in 1998 polarised the community in Squamish. There was definitely an air of mistrust and tension about the place in the aftermath of Bob's death.

For a few years my dad and Katy didn't speak. She had written some harsh things about his family - deserved in my case, but unwarranted in dad's. Katy criticised dad's behaviour when he arrived back in Squamish, insinuating that dad was implying Bob might have suffered a heart attack, like his father. He wasn't. For a start dad had been in an information vacuum for four days. There was no internet back then. Imagine the thoughts that must have been going through his head as he waited for the connecting flights from Mexico to Vancouver. As soon as he got home he had to act both as my father and the McIntosh's family doctor. It was a horrendous situation made all the more distressing by the fact Bob was also a good friend. Katy and dad reconciled a few years later.

Of course, I should have been keeping my head down during this time, staying out of trouble and sorting out my shit. The police were out to get me. I may have been innocent of any involvement in Bob's death but they were itching to take me down because of my reputation. I handed them the opportunity in May 1998.

Cat Lake is one of the most popular camping destinations in British Columbia. It's a few kilometres north of Squamish and attracts visitors from the town and as far afield as Vancouver. It's a stunning spot. Beautiful crystal blue water to swim in, and a maze of hiking and biking trails encompassing the lake. There are quite a few camping sites at Cat Lake and it gets really busy in the peak months

The summer season starts at the end of May, on the Victoria Day holiday, which is the long weekend at the end of each May. Me and a group of buddies went up to Cat Lake to party on the Friday evening. I had my girlfriend with me, and Ryan McMillan was also there with his girlfriend. To reach the lake you turn off the highway, bump along a logging road for a couple of kms and then you reach a parking lot. Then it's a short hike to the lake.

A few of us went off in search of a good spot to camp and a few minutes later the rest of our group arrived, among them my girlfriend. She was pissed off because there's been a slight collision in the parking lot and her rear-view mirror was smashed. I asked if she'd got the other driver's insurance details. She hadn't so I suggested we head back to the lot, swap details and then return to party. Ryan McMillan came with us because he'd forgotten a cooler in the trunk of his car.

It was uphill back to the lot, past some designated camping spots that were on a series of raised plateaus cut into the hillside. Passing one campsite we saw a group of guys throwing bottles down the hill into the woods. Now those bottles were going to either smash or land on campers down below. Ryan and I went to have a word and told them to stop throwing the bottles. They promised they would.

We weren't at the parking lot for long. We exchanged insurance details, Ryan got the cooler and we headed back down the hill. By now we'd been joined by a few of our buddies, who had just arrived. As we passed the campsite these out-of-town guys were still chucking bottles. We yelled at them to cut it out and this time they told us to 'fuck off'. We weren't having that. In we charged and these guys - there were 16 of them, according to subsequent press reports - fronted up. They had shovels and logs. We had a cooler and logs. We just hoed into them. One big brawl. Apparently four of them were carted off to hospital with various injuries - broken bones, smashed teeth, gashed legs. It was a brutal fight. I got whacked over the head with a shovel but when the dust settled we were the ones standing. We threw most of their shit on their fire and told them to fuck off back to the city because they didn't know how to treat the countryside properly. That was it. We thought that was the end of it and went back to the rest of our group.

But these guys went straight to the police and cried 'racist attack'. Within a matter of hours I was picked up and being a holiday weekend I spent four days in custody. The newspapers went to town. 'Cudmore in racist attack' and all these bullshit headlines. I'm not denying that racist words were used - on both sides - but the fight started because they were hurling bottles through the woods. We didn't attack them because there were Canadian Filipinos. They called us 'fucking Rednecks', we called them 'Fucking Filipinos' but they tried to make out we told them to 'fuck off home'. We did say that - by home we meant Vancouver not the Philipines. We didn't want city boys trashing our lake.

Certain sections of the media tried to run with the racist angle despite the fact the Squamish Royal Canadian Mounted Police investigated and dismissed the claims that racism was a factor. It was a brawl between two groups of teenagers. One side lost and couldn't accept it. There was a lot of misinformation in how the press reported the fight, mainly because they only got one side of the story. For example, the Canadian Filipinos guys said they were attacked by 30 youths, presumably because their pride couldn't deal with the fact they'd outnumbered us two to one. For many in Squamish my involvement was the last straw. I was charged with actual bodily harm - I was the only one charged as a result of the fight - my name was dragged through the gutter. There was a youth rally denouncing violence a couple of weeks later and I was regular in the letters' page of the local paper. One, written by the Filipino-Canadian Youth Alliance, said the Cat Lake fight "is a shining example of the racism that is entrenched in small communities and cities all B.C."

It was bullshit but sometimes bullshit sticks. But that was when the Squamish Nation reached out to me in way I'll never forget. A letter appeared in the local paper, the Squamish Chief, written by Maya Joseph, a representative of the Squamish Nation. This is what she wrote:

"I am not writing this letter to defend any acts of violence, however I write in disbelief

that a group of Squamish youth intentionally planned out this rampage. Like many of you who have lived in this community for a long time. I can recall Jamie's past brushes with the law. And like you, I didn't know him but I heard a lot about him.

"When I heard he was back in town a couple of years ago after serving his time in camps and jails, I was frightened. I was frightened because I thought what if my teenage sons encountered him. And guess what? They did. What surprised me was that this encounter was friendly, however as a parent, I still worried.

"My children taught me a valuable lesson. They said: 'Mom, Jamie's a different person. He's mellowed out. You shouldn't judge him if you don't know him. People should give him another chance. Just because he's big, it doesn't mean he's a mean person'. And so I took my children's words because I trusted them. I decided to give Jamie Cudmore the benefit of a doubt.

"Over the last two years of getting to know Jamie, I could not believe that this was the same young man that our community made him out to be. Yes, just his mere size was intimidating and downright frightening. But no, he wasn't a bully. He treated my sons with utmost respect.

"Last year Jamie joined my son's lacrosse team. The North Shore Indians was primarily an all-native team with the exception of two non-natives. One of them was Jamie. Like hockey, fights often occurred. I've seen Jamie casually walking away from a fight not wanting to jeopardize his teammates or the game. He showed a great respect for First Nations and participated in pre-game rituals that included native smudges and prayers to the Great Spirit. He attended Pow Wows with the team members and spoke of learning the Squamish language at the Totem Nursery School on the Stawamus Reserve. He often came to my home and always showed respect for our native culture. This was the side of him that came through. Only because I took the chance to know him more deeply. Jamie Cudmore a racist? A radical white supremacist? I hardly think so."

I'll always be indebted to Maya for writing that letter.

I'm thankful, too, with the mature hindsight of adulthood, that the people of Squamish didn't shun my dad. It would have been easy to lump all the Cudmores together. They didn't. They saw there was only one jerk among us, and that was me. My dad received a huge amount of support and understanding from his friends and patients. I know that meant a great deal to him. He was at his wit's end trying to deal with me, and it would have made life even more unbearable if people had turned their back on him.

In recent years dad's told me that through it all he never felt ashamed of the family name. He knew that at heart I was a good kid. So did most people in Squamish. As Maya said in her letter, most of the time I was polite and respectful, certainly always towards my dad's friends and acquaintances. It was only among my peer group that I displayed a Jekyll and Hyde character.

Nonetheless some people wanted to see me punished, and they got their wish when I appeared in court a few weeks after the fight. I remember walking into the dock and facing me were the Filipino guys, all sitting in the front row, trying to stare me down.

I'd been charged with three counts of assault but two were dropped. On the outstanding charge I pleaded guilty. I knew I was going down, all that remained was to hear the length of the sentence. Four months with 18 months probation. The judge also ordered me to have no contact with seven individuals, my buddies, and to enrol on an anger management course. As I was led from the dock, an anger management course was the least of my concerns.

I was 19, no longer a juvenile, so I was going to prison. I was sent to Fraser Regional Correction Centre in Maple Ridge, 50km east of Vancouver. It 's what they call a multi-security level prison, which means there are prisoners on remand, awaiting their trial, and also inmates categorised as 'open', 'medium' and 'secure'. I spent my time in my cell, working out or occasionally involved on one of the work programmes, such as maintaining the grounds or cleaning the block. We got a few dollars for that sort of work, which we used to buy extra food.

It's the lack of privacy that gets to you in prison. Everything is filmed and there are no real dead spots, and there always guards around. I had no trouble, either from other inmates or the guards. If you didn't go looking for trouble you were O.K.

You are forced to adapt in prison. Suddenly you are no longer in control of your life. You eat when you're told and you eat what is in front of you. You exercise at a set time, you are locked up for the night at a set time, you live your life according to another set of rules. It's quite an adjustment to make because in everyday life we have so much choice and going to prison it's suddenly taken from you. That's the key to surviving prison, you just succumb to the system and wait out your time. You fill your days as best you can and look forward to the day you get back your freedom. But I can see how some people become serial offenders and almost prefer prison to civilian life. You can become institutionalised and when you're released and the routine is no longer there some people can't cope with fending for themselves.

Not me, though. For a start there wasn't enough to eat and the beds aren't exactly the best. At Fraser they were plastic cots that hung from the wall and my feet dangled over the edge.

Fraser Regional was also a shock for mum and dad. My previous incarcerations had been in youth detention facilities, more wilderness camps than prisons. Visiting involved a lot of travelling but at least the destination wasn't sinister. Dad always came to visit because he wanted me to know I hadn't been abandoned even though to see me at Camp Trapping had meant flying to Prince George. Mum found it harder. She suffered terribly from stress, believing she'd failed as a parent. Visiting me, seeing me locked up, was too much for her.

But was my dad was visibly shaken the first time he came to visit me in Fraser Regional. It was like the movies. The uniformed guards and the clanging of heavy iron doors. It brought home to him the depth of my fall. It was on one of these visits, perhaps the first one, perhaps another, I can't remember, that my dad looked me in the eyes and told me he would never stop loving me. But he couldn't love some of the things I did and he couldn't continue to be supportive if I kept doing these things. The word my dad uses when he talks about this period isn't 'anger', it's 'sadness'. He was desperately sad that his son seemed determined to waste his life opportunities.

It wasn't long before I was back in court on two charges of assault, stemming from a fight the previous November. I was held on remand while the further investigations were held, so back I went to Fraser Regional. I was there for several more months. A birthday passed (my twentieth) a Christmas, and a New Year began. Like I said at the start, one thing prison has going for it is that it allows you a lot of time to reflect on where your life's gone wrong.

It didn't require much reflection to understand that 1998 had been the worst year of my life. Somehow I had to turn my life around. Mum and dad had done plenty of tough talking with me down the years, and they'd also shown enormous love and support. They'd done everything they could to get me on the right track, but it was up to me to change. I had to stop being a prick and start being responsible. I remember mum saying once that my problem was I fought my buddies' battles for them. They egged me on because were either too scared or too weak to front up themselves. If I didn't want to spend my life going back and forth to prison, I had to escape this downward spiral of violence.

Easier said than done. But in prison I saw one possible escape route. I'd started playing rugby a couple of years earlier for the Squamish Axemen, my local team. That gave me an outlet for my physicality and I'd also glimpsed, even at that very amateur level, that rugby was a tough sport played by tough men, but there were rules, discipline and teamwork that if followed brought success. I thought back to my time at Camp Trapping. Hadn't that had the same ethos? And hadn't I thrived in the environment?

I realised that me and rugby were made for each other. Here was a sport where I could charge about, let off steam, crash into people, but within a set of strict rules. Rugby allowed me to channel my aggression and energy in a positive direction. There was also the camaraderie. I liked being in a gang for that reason but the fellowship of a street gang is superficial. What are you working towards? Usually towards breaking the law.

I wouldn't say I had an epiphany in prison. I didn't wake up one morning and jump out of bed with the fervour of a born-again Christian. It was the culmination of a lot of analysis and soul-searching. I'd caused mum and especially dad so much unhappiness, I'd brought shame on the family name, probably caused a lot of shit at school for my brothers, and for that I was truly sorry. But the prime motivator was the realisation that I didn't want to ruin my life. We only get one shot at it, so let's make it a good one.

The day before I was due back in court to answer the assault charges I was released. It all happened very quickly and to this day I'm not sure of the legal arguments that led to the decision to drop the charges. I'd known from the start that the prosecutor hated my guts from day one and was determined to see me convicted, but it seemed eventually the Crown realised they couldn't proceed on lack of evidence. Whatever. All I cared about was the fact I was getting the hell out of Fraser Regional.

It was an emotional twenty four hours, from learning the charges had been dropped to actually walking out of prison a free man. When I did leave - this would have been the spring of 1999 - I made a vow that I would never be back. Mum was waiting and she drove me to Trout Lake Park in Vancouver. I walked into the changing room and there were all my buddies from the Squamish Axemen Rugby Club. Here was my new 'gang'.

Chapter five

I was about 15 when I picked up a rugby ball for the first time. We had a few coaching sessions at Brackendale high school. I enjoyed it, though the greatest buzz was seeing how proud my old man was. I knew rugby was 'his sport'. He'd told me some tales of when he played in England and one of the rituals of the Cudmore house in the late 1980s and early 1990s was watching the Five Nations together on TV. Even during the worst excesses of my teenage years, rugby was one way I could bond with my dad.

I was fortunate that as I began to take an interest in rugby the Squamish Axemen club was formed. The driving force behind the Axemen was Greg Richmond. He was the club president and he injected a fair amount of his own cash to get the Axemen off the ground. Greg was a successful local businessman whose company GBA Logging, was a big employer in the local area.

In fact Greg gave me my first job in the industry in the 1990s and that's how I came to play for the Axemen. I should probably say a quick word about my days logging, to lay to rest once and for all the myth that I was lumberjack. I've had a few nicknames over the : 'Cuddles' being one, 'Le Bucheron' another. I never actually wore a checked shirt, wielded an axe and went around chopping down trees! It was less glamorous than that.

I started logging when I was in my teens, working around Squamish and further north, up in Pemberton and in the Elaho Valley. Most days I worked with Dave Stewart, a great guy who's still in the industry and doing well for himself on Vancouver Island. As loggers our job was to remove the trees from the forest. So we would be sent to a site where 30 or 40 acres of trees had been taken down by the fallers. A big steel tower would be erected with cables that ran up the hill to the logs. We wrapped chokers round the logs and then they were dragged up to the yarding machines which loaded them onto trucks for delivery to the saw mills.

It was hard, dangerous work. I knew a few guys who suffered nasty injuries logging. Getting hands trapped in the cables is an occupational hazard but the fatal accidents usually occur when trees roll and turn. It was a rolling log that nearly cost Dave his head. We were getting these logs off the hill and one was horizontal, so we were turning it vertical, as they should be when they come down the hill. The danger lies in the logs bending as they're moved from the horizontal to the vertical, and then suddenly springing free, ripping off the cables as they hurtle down the hillside. This is what happened on this day. There was a 'whoosh', and Dave turned to see a twenty metre baseball bat heading his way at a hell of a speed. He just had time to duck. Just as well, really, or his head would have scored a home run.

Not that we were spooked by such incidents. It was all part of the fun! When you're 17 you think you're invincible, right? One game Dave and I liked to play was 'Run or Die'. In logging we used hand-held horn blasts, known in the trade as 'bugs', to communicate with the yarding machine down at the bottom of landing. Once we had fastened the chokers round the logs, we would sound the horn and that was the signal for the yarding machine to haul down the logs on these long steel cable, which were around 500 metres in length. To play Run or Die, Dave and I would leave the horn on the stump of a tree and then on the count of three, run in to a log each, pull the cables in as fast as we could, wrap then around our respective logs and then sprint back to the 'bug' and give it a couple of blasts. Whoever did that first was the winner. If you were the loser, you just had to hope you weren't still fiddling around with the cable. And if you were you'd have to move real quick or else you'd go for a ride down the hill with the log. My days logging were some of the happiest of my life. Dave and I were like kids running wild in the woods. We worked hard but we didn't think of it as work. I've always felt at ease in the wilderness. It's an environment I respect but don't fear. I suppose, too, I began logging at a time in my life when I was getting into trouble with the law so it was an almost an escape, to head into the wilderness and channel my energy into logging.

But to get back to the rugby. Greg Richmond launched the Squamish Axemen in the mid-1990s, and invited me and Dave to come along. I remember his sales pitch was along the lines of "You can get up to the same bullshit that you do in the bar each night but you won't get into any trouble'. Who could resist that offer? Greg was player, president, coach, one of the good old boys from Squamish who's still logging. Tough old bastard. By now he must be held together by bootlaces.

There'd been a few half-hearted attempts over the years to get a rugby club off the ground in Squamish, relying on the handful of British expatriates in the region and also the odd Kiwi and Aussie living in Whistler. Greg was determined that this time the Squamish Axemen would thrive, and in 1995 we played our first match in Division Four of the Vancouver Rugby League.

The team was a mix of veterans, guys like Greg, Tom Braidwood and Brian Bucholz and then youngsters like me, Dave and Trevor Midgely.

The fiercest matches were against Capilanos and Gibson's Pigs. The Caps came from Vancouver, and recruited a lot of players from the North Shore High Schools, where wrestling was pretty big. So they were tough. But they were city boys all the same. Those matches never lacked for big fights and big hits.

The Piggies hailed from just across the water. Their official name was Gibsons Rugby and Athletic Club - but everyone called them the 'Piggies'. Most of the Piggies were loggers and so like the Axemen they were looked down on by the Vancouver Rugby Union. That created a bond between us, though you wouldn't have known it to see us play.

Their clubhouse was built on Armour's Beach and, strapping several logs together, they'd created a boom on the water. This was the setting for their rookie initiation, mandatory for any Pig or any opponent playing their first match at their ground. The rookie was thrown a pair of logging boots - usually five sizes too big or too small - and once on they stood on the starting line. As soon as the clock started the rookie had to skull a beer, sprint round the boom, skull another beer and only then did the clock stop.

When it was the turn of me and Dave, we declined the offer of a pair of logging boots. We had our own in the back of Greg's van. Needless to say we both smashed the Piggies' world record for the Rookie Initiation - one of my proudest feats!

Those days playing for the Axemen were awesome. Amateur club rugby has a unique charm. There's nothing glamorous about it - I remember quite a few matches when we changed in a parking lot, some of the boys smoking as they did so - but it's fun and there are no egos. Just 15 guys playing for each other.

It was thanks to rugby that I made the front page of the Squamish Chief in October 1996 - just about the only time during my teens that I appeared in my local paper for a reason other than a run-in with the police. There was a big photo of me jumping in the line-out during a match against the Capilanos. It would take me nearly three more years to appreciate what rugby could offer me, and when I did it was the Capilanos who helped bring out my talent.

*

After my release from prison I played a few games for the Axemen but by now I knew that if I wanted to really leave my troubled past behind I had also to leave Squamish behind. A couple of guys from the Axemen had moved to Vancouver and joined the Rowing Club rugby club. When I moved to the city in the summer of 1999 they invited me to one of their training sessions at the Brockton Oval in Stanley Park. It's a hell of a beautiful ground, and they were welcoming, but it just wasn't me. I was still logging at that time and I drove down to training on a Tuesday evening, still in my grimy logging gear, and I remember walking into the changing room and seeing the boys taking off their suits after a hard day in the office. The training went well, I enjoyed that aspect of it, and they had me starting at No8 on the weekend. I had a beer with them afterwards in the clubhouse and they were nice enough. But I just didn't feel comfortable. I was out of my element. Nevertheless I decided to give it another crack on Thursday but en route to the ground I stopped for gas at West Vancouver. While I was filling up my van with gas I saw a guy I knew who was on his way to Capilanos for training. He invited me along and I laughed in his face. "No way I'm going to Caps not after all the fights I had playing for the Axemen". But he talked me round. Why not? I thought.

So I went down to Capilanos and straight away found it more me. It was representative of all walks of life, and within 30 minutes I was carrying the nickname 'Squamish', because the Capilanos boys thought it hilarious that an Axeman would cross to the dark side.

Capilanos were, and still are, one of the biggest and most prestigious rugby clubs in Canada. Even back in 1999 they had a mini section, women's rugby teams, ran several senior sides and they were a great example of a community club. It was completely different to what I'd known at the Axemen. There we had played our matches on high school pitches and we were lucky if fifteen guys turned up to training; at Caps there were around sixty at my first training session.

About a month after I joined Capilanos I was invited to go on tour to California. We had a whale of a time, playing matches in Los Angeles, San Diego and San Francisco. One night we found ourselves in a nightclub in Anaheim, just outside L.A, and some of the boys spotted Dennis Rodman in the V.I.P section. He was playing for the L.A Lakers at this time, though by then his basketball career was overshadowed by his off-court antics. But he was pretty cool, waving us into the VIP section and the next thing we know we're on our way to his place on Long beach to continue the party. But when we arrived at Rodman's place the party was well and truly out of control. That guy is something else. We slipped away and got the hell out of there.

The tour to California was another significant moment in my life, from a sporting and personal perspective. It opened my eyes to the opportunities on offer if I really started taking rugby seriously. I could travel places, expand my mind, broaden my horizons. Returning to Vancouver, I packed in my logging work and took up the offer of a job in the construction industry from the Dakotas, a large construction firm in Vancouver that had links to Capilanos. That provided me financial stability and also began to instil in me a work ethic. Because those days on the construction site were tough. We'd started at six in the morning and often not finish till nine at night. But the pay was good and the work satisfying. More important the work, and the rugby, helped me steer clear of some of my old buddies from Squamish who were now living in Vancouver. One Squamish boy I did hang out with was Steve Featherstone. Like me he was in the city to start afresh. In his case by boxing. We worked together for a time on the construction site and he ended up boxing for British Columbia at the Canada Games. He's now pretty big in the construction industry and I'm proud to call him my friend.

Soon I moved out of my mum's place, where I'd been staying since leaving Squamish, and managed to get in a house with some of the Cap boys. It was fraternity living. Five or six guys in the house, playing rugby, working hard and partying at the weekend. I partied as hard as I worked but at that age the body is a sponge, right? You push yourself to the limits in everything and get the next morning feeling no different. Oh, to be young again!

My rugby was really beginning to improve at Capilanos. I was playing in the back-row, usually at 6, sometimes at No8, and I ended up winning Capilanos' Rookie of the Year award for the 1999-2000 season. But my rugby was still very rough round the edges. I needed a challenge, a really tough one, to smooth down some of those edges, and in rugby what's more of a challenge than going to New Zealand?

Chapter Six

I have Bob Bremner to thank for my season in New Zealand. He was one of the good old boys at Capilanos, one of those no-nonsense centres who always did the basics to perfection, and he also worked in construction industry. Bob told me about the Stormy exchange programme between the Capilano club and East Coast Bays in New Zealand. The programme gave players the opportunity to spend a season in another culture, playing - in the case of us Canadians - a far superior standard of rugby. Bob had spent quite a bit of time in New Zealand (and had even found himself a Kiwi wife) and he encouraged me to give it a go. I wasn't too keen on settling down with a wife at that moment in time but from a rugby viewpoint I thought it made sense. I also liked the sound of the club. East Coast Bays is on the North Shore of Auckland and is a member of the North Harbour Rugby Union. From what Bob said, it had a similar ethos to Capilanos - a real community club for blue-collar workers

So I sold my truck, bought a plane ticket to Auckland, and off I went to New Zealand for their 2000-01 season. I landed at 6.30 on a Saturday morning and waiting for me was Bruce Wigglesworth. But there was a problem. I'd arrived but my baggage had got stuck in L.A. Not a problem, said Bruce, who turned out to be the best contact I could have wished for. Having gently informed me that I was playing that afternoon, he showed me to my flat, lent me some kit and later that day collected me and drove me to the game.

I won't forget my first taste of New Zealand rugby in a hurry. We played Northcote and the difference in skill level and speed was incredible. It took only a few minutes to learn what happened in New Zealand if you got caught on the wrong side of a ruck. It was a real eye-opener, a little daunting, even. But that's why I'd come to East Coast Bays.

It was at the Bays that I began my transition from the back-row to the second-row. The club, like all Kiwi clubs, had a surfeit of class loose forwards, and so I moved into the second row where they thought my size and strength could be most effective. I was fine with the switch. I'd been playing rugby for four years and most of my new teammates had picked up a rugby ball before they'd learned to walk. So I just did what I was told and watched, listened and learned.

I'd recommend a season in New Zealand for any young aspiring player. There is no better place to develop your rugby education. My game improved dramatically, all facets, but asked to choose I'd say it was my reading of the game that benefited most from my time at the Bays. But my skill levels also came on in leaps and bounds. In

Canada it was truck it up and off we go again, but in New Zealand they executed all these skills at high intensity and, for example, it was a given that you could pass off both hands so that was an aspect of my game which I worked hard to improve. The physical side of the game was fine. I was as fit and as strong as the Kiwis, but it was the gulf in skill levels that needed bridging.

Away from the rugby field I had a great time. In fact it was a home from home for me. On the north shore of Auckland I found a very similar way of life - and mentality - to where I'd grown up. It was an outdoor life - there was even some logging not far from where I was living - and I was able to go surfing and hunting. The people share many of the same traits as the west coast of Canada: straight-talking and down-to-earth.

I was asked to stay in New Zealand but while I was weighing up the invitation I got called back to Vancouver by Dave Clark, then the head coach of the Canada national set-up. He wanted to integrate me in the Pacific Pride squad. That signalled that I was edging close to winning a senior cap. Much as I loved New Zealand I knew I had to head home and try and get my hands on a cap. It was tough to leave the Bays but I would be reunited with one of my teammates a few years later when I signed for Grenoble and found myself packing down once more with Tongan lock Alifeleti Fakaongo.

*

The Pacific Pride U23 squad was an idea of Dave Clark's, bringing together the best young players from the west coast of Canada and developing them in a professional environment. Dave is an Aussie, and he brought a huge amount of experience and intelligence to his coaching. He'd been on the periphery of the Wallaby squad in the 1970s, without ever winning a cap, and after several years as the Head Coach of rugby at the Australian Institute for Sport in Canberra, he came to Canada in the mid-1990s. Initially he was responsible for the Commonwealth Centre rugby programme in Victoria, but in 1999 he was appointed the first professional head coach of Canada

The Pacific Pride XV played in Canada's Premier League, which 15 years ago was a far better standard than today. Now, most of the best young Canadian players, play in Europe but in 2002 only a handful such as Morgan Williams and Dan Baugh played for big European clubs.

When I joined the Pacific Pride set-up there were players like Ryan Smith, Matt King, Dave Moonlight and Derek Daypuck, all of whom would go on to establish themselves in the national side. Dave Moonlight, in particular, was a hell of a player, who should have won more caps than he did. He was a winger, tough and fast, and in recent seasons I've played alongside his cousin, John, several times for Canada. Daypuck, 'Puckers', is another who I enjoyed playing with, so I hope he doesn't mind me mentioning his claim to fame. We were playing for Canada against England in 2004 at Twickenham. That's right, the home of rugby, the most venerable stadium in the world. Canada were awarded a penalty so up stepped Puckers to kick the ball into touch. But he sliced the ball so badly that it actually went backwards and we lost ground. He claims the camera angle made it look worse than it was. Whatever you say, Puckers...

The Pacific Pride programme was another significant part of my education. I've already described how the season in East Coast Bays improved my game; now I was able to return to Canada and hone those skills in a professional environment. We were coached daily, received video analysis, given specific fitness and weights programmes and educated about nutrition and looking after our bodies in general. Soon I stopped doing even part-time construction work in Vancouver and relocated to Victoria, where the Pacific Pride were based. Dave Clark and John MacMillan, who was one of the coaches, and is now the President of PacificSport Victoria, were instrumental in turning me from an enthusiastic amateur into a focused professional. I sometimes had to pinch myself to believe it was all really happening. Two years earlier I'd just been released from prison and now here I was playing representative rugby under the eye of Canada's top coaches. The past was well and truly behind me and the future was boundless - but what I wanted above all else was my first cap for Canada.

In April 2002 I was selected to tour Germany with the Canada Under 23 squad. We played four matches, starting with a 71-0 win against Bavaria but we then lost our second game 18-17 to North Germany. That proved to be our only defeat and we ended the tour with a 20-14 victory over the German national side at Heidelberg. A few of us stayed on in Germany and got a train to Prague. At least, that was the intention. Me, Pat Flack and Scott Franklin boarded the train, found an empty compartment, and made ourselves snug with a case of German beer. When we arrived at the Czech border, a couple of policemen came into the compartment asking to see our passports. I was travelling on my British one, so they had no problem with that, but Pat and Scott had only Canadian passports. So they were hauled off the train at gunpoint. I thought about staying put and finishing the beer, but I got off , too, and we were all returned to Germany.

I was back in Canada to play for Canada West against a strong Scotland side who were touring the country. That was a big day for me, the clearest indication yet that I was close to winning a full cap. Canada West, as the name suggests, was a representative side featuring players from the west coast. Most were young guys, and I was packing down alongside a Capilano teammate, Ron Johnstone and there a couple of other Caps in the side in flanker Mike Andrew and my buddy, Bob Bremner, in the centre. We were captained by Mark Lawson, a tireless hooker, who I would play with many times for Canada in the years to come.

It was the third match of the Scots' tour and they'd had little trouble beating Canada East (38-8) and an unofficial Canada XV (33-8). We knew we had to tear into them from the start, stop them getting any rhythm. The match was at Centennial Stadium in Victoria, and for me personally, it was the biggest game of my career to date. It was a young but good Scotland side. The great Ian McGeechan was coach and several members of the squad like Steve Brotherstone, Gordon Bulloch and Andrew Henderson had played in the recent Six Nations.

It was the boot of their fly-half, Gordon Ross, that proved decisive. He kicked three penalties and pinned us back with some canny tactical kicking when our pack was on top. The only try of the game was scored by their prop, Allan Jacobson, but if Mike Danskin hadn't had an off-day with the boot, missing three penalties in the second-half, Canada West would have claimed a famous scalp. It was a match in which I showed my good and bad sides. To quote one match report: "Cudmore made a tremendous play near the halfway line - dropping on a chipped ball and then counter attacking with great affect." But in the next sentence: "Scotland then appeared to have scored a try in the 70th minute - but [referee] Kuklinski had instead called Cudmore for stomping - sending the beefy forward off with a yellow card. "

From the penalty I conceded, Ross kicked into our corner and Jacobsen then drove over from the lineout for the crucial try. Those 60 seconds encapsulated the strengths and weaknesses of my game. Two years of intensive rugby in New Zealand and then with the Pacific Pride had smoothed off a lot of my technical rough edges. I was a good ball-carrier, athletic in the loose, powerful in defence and my set-piece contribution was strong. My temperament was the chink in my armour and there's no doubt the coaching staff were concerned I could become a liability the higher up the representative ladder I climbed. Dave Clarke, the national coach, talked to me about it and obviously I didn't want him to think of me as a loose cannon. I had my eyes on that first cap and after all the hard work I'd put in over the last few years I knew I had to work on tightening self-control.

Whatever I promised Clarkie, it had its desired effect. On July 13 2002 I won my first cap. It's the most special moment in every rugby player's career, to play for your country, and I was on a high for about a month afterwards. Almost exactly four years earlier was life was at rock bottom. I'd just been sentenced to four months' prison for assault and now I was an international rugby player. It had been a hell of a journey, and I'd succeeded only because of the love and support of my family and friends, and the encouragement of all the boys at Capilanos.

The match itself was against the USA - who better to make your debut against, if you're Canadian, than the old enemy? - and the venue was the Rockne Stadium in

Chicago. That was an experience. I was nervous enough as it was, and the bus ride to the ground didn't exactly leave me relaxed. The neighbourhood around the Rockne Stadium wasn't the best back then. Six storey brownstone houses and burned-out cars all around. Then suddenly on a street corner there would be a pristine white Cadillac surrounded by a gang of desperate-looking people. What could possibly be for sale...?

I only got on for a few minutes at the end of the match, by which time Canada were way out of sight. It was a very strong Canadian side, captained by the great Al Charron, and featuring a number of grizzled veterans such as Rod Snow, Mike James and Winston Stanley. They all had the respect of the younger guys but they never abused it. They were approachable and down-to-earth, and any questions we younger guys had they would answer. In Mike's case, too much. Boy, he sure likes to talk. Morgan Williams nicknamed Mike 'quarter' because if asked him for his two cents' worth of advice, he'd give you 25.

Two tries in the first-half from centre Marco Di Girolamo killed off the American challenge, and we ran out 36-13 winners. The win all but sealed our place in the 2003 World Cup and after the match Charron presented me and Matt King, a Pacific Pride teammate, with our Canada caps.

Not that I had long to savour my new-found status as an international rugby player. Next up for Canada was a tour to South America to play two more World Cup qualifiers. The first was against Uruguay in Montevideo and it was the scene of one of the great - how can I put this without being sued - accidental officiating blunders in rugby history! We were leading 23-22 but in the final quarter Uruguay were awarded a penalty wide out. I was on the bench so had a pretty good view from behind their goalkicker. I breathed a sigh of relief as I watched the ball sail about three metres to the right of the post. Next thing I know the touch judges - who I believe were local - raised their flags. Like I said, a complete accident on their part...

The Uruguay Test was my initiation in South American rugby and it was an eye-opener compared to what I'd experienced in New Zealand, Germany and Australia. 'Passionate' is one word you could use to describe their fans. There are several others, which I muttered to myself as we were pelted with everything from oranges to car batteries as we ran out onto the pitch. If I'd known what it would be like sitting on the bench, I would have brought an umbrella to shield me from all the spittle directed our way from the spectators.

From Uruguay we travelled to Chile but not before I spent on one of the most fascinating afternoons of my life in the company of Doctor Roberto Canessa. He was one of the survivors from the Andes air disaster of 1972 rugby team, a member of Montevideo's Old Christians Club, whose plane crashed en route from Uruguay to Santiago. Roberto told the squad about the crash and how he and others survived for 72 days in the mountains, resorting to eat the flesh of the dead to stay alive. I reckon he talked for about an hour and a half, and in that time no one moved a muscle. It was an extraordinary and inspiring experience.

I made my first start for Canada against Chile, locking the scrum alongside Ron Johnstone, my buddy from Capilanos and Canada West. It was another mixed bag from me, a performance that did little to allay Dave Clarke's concerns about my temperament. Eight minutes into the second half I was sent to the sin bin for using an elbow in a tackle. Chile converted the penalty but at least my indiscretion had little outcome on this occasion on the match with Canada winning 29-11. Nonetheless it was frustrating for Dave Clarke, and for me. I was developing a reputation for ill-discipline, and worse, giving away kickable penalties. With the 2003 World Cup just 12 months away I was in danger of being overlooked if I couldn't tighten my discipline. I had to be set an example, taught how the world's best players carry themselves, and what better place to learn than Wales?

Chapter seven

I scored a try on my debut for Llanelli Scarlets. But to be honest just about everyone in the team scored a try that day. We thrashed Slovenia 127-7 on a pre-season tour . It was probably the most one-sided match I've ever played but nonetheless the Scarlets tour was another notch in my progression.

I joined Llanelli in the summer of 2002, actually coming over between winning my first cap and going to South America to play Uruguay and Chile. I had Pat Dunkley, the Canada hooker, to thank for getting me a shot at the Scarlets. He spent the 2001-02 season playing for Swansea and it was with his help, and his agent's, that the opportunity arose at the Scarlets.

I was still fresh-faced in the rugby world so the opportunity to sign my first professional contract with a club as big as the Scarlets was huge. I remember looking around the changing room on my first day and everywhere were **Welsh Test stars, British Lions legends, American and Tongan internationals - all pretty daunting for a kid just setting out in the rugby world.**

We only played one match in Slovenia but nonetheless the mini tour was a great initiation to professional rugby. I remember one evening strolling through town and thinking 'Gee, life's pretty good'. I'm a professional rugby player with my own club car, I've played for Canada, and now I'm touring a country where all the women are beautiful!

Gareth Jenkins was coach when I arrived at the Scarlets, and I didn't really have much to do with him because I was very much on the edge of the squad. I was just running around at 100mph as the new kid on the block, trying to impress him and the rest of the boys. I'm more of a watcher than an asker so I scrutinised everyone and everything around me, absorbing all the advice, and trying to emulate things that I thought would benefit my game. In that respect Scott Quinnell was a huge help. He was a bit of a hero of mine, a legend in both rugby union and rugby league - and I learned so much from observing how he trained and worked on his skills, and how he conducted himself as a professional athlete. Socially, I hung out with Chris Wyatt, staying true to the second row union. Chris is one of the most affable guys you could wish to meet.

My opportunities were limited for the Scarlets. I was competing for a place in the second row against Chris, Vernon Cooper and the veteran American Luke Gross, so while I got a few runs I was far from a regular. I did, however, make the first of my 47 Champions Cup appearances (or the Heineken Cup as it was called back then) in the colours of the Scarlets, coming on as a substitute against Glasgow in January 2003. I wasn't on for long, and we were cruising to a comfortable 34-8 victory thanks in no small part to a hat-trick of tries from wing Garan Evans. It was a bit of a last-minute call-up. Vernon Cooper withdrew with an injury on the eve of the match, so Gross moved up off the bench and I was brought into the squad. If you'd had told me that day that ten years later I would be starting a European Cup Final - and for a French side - I would never have believed you.

I was living in Llanelli and training every day with the Scarlets but because of my

limited playing time for them a solution was devised. I was loaned out to Llandovery. Where? I'd never heard of the place. They were an amateur club playing in the Welsh first division, and the town was about fifty miles north-east of Llanelli on the edge of the Brecon Beacons national park. In other words it was out in the sticks, and for a country boy like myself it was perfect.

I had the best time ever in Llandovery. What a bunch of boys! At my first training session all the line-out calls were in Welsh. It was a tradition, they told me, so I'd better start learning the language. Have you heard Welsh being spoken? Fortunately they couldn't keep a straight face for more than a hour or so, and to my great relief they admitted they'd just wanted to wind up the wet-behind-the-ears Canadian boy!

I still keep in touch with a lot of them, and a group came to France last year to watch me play my final match for Clermont. I invited them back to the Cudmore ranch afterwards and we had a few bottles of wine and reminisced about the good old days.

The rugby at Llanelli was good. It was hard, too. My first match was away at Aberavon, which is on the outskirts of Port Talbot and its giant steelworks. I remember sitting on the bus on the way to the ground, thinking 'Heck, people actually live here?' They did, and the rugby club was one of their few distractions. So there was quite a crowd and they all wanted to see the farming boys of Llandovery get a good kicking. One of the Aberavon pack thought he was the world's hardest man. He was putting himself about, trying to bully us. As I've said, back in those days I wasn't always the coolest customer, so when I could take no more of it I threw him to the ground and told him to cut out the rough stuff. He didn't really take much notice.

On the bus back to Llandovery Matthew Monaghan had a quiet word, explained that I had to impose myself more in Welsh rugby. Matt's a great guy so I heeded his advice. The next Saturday I found myself up against not just one, but two, self-styled tough guys. When they came at us fists flying I knocked them both out. Llandovery seemed happy. I was learning fast.

I was the tallest and the heaviest in the team but I was playing alongside some tough men. My second row for the season was Arwel Davies, a milk farmer, and though he was only about 1m 91cm and 96 kilos he had the raw strength of someone brought up outdoors. Once he got his hands on the ball you didn't get it back.

But they weren't all farming boys. Matthew Monaghan worked with young adults with learning difficulties and every now and again he'd bring a group up to training. The moment they saw the rugby ball their faces lit up and we'd get them involved in the practise drills. They were good days. It was demanding, though, dividing my time between two clubs. On one occasion I played the second half for the Scarlets in Edinburgh on a Friday night, and then as soon as the match was over I drove down to Llandovery and played 80 minutes at Pontypool. Ponty put 60 points on us - but I don't think I was totally to blame!

But I did have time to let my hair down during my season in Wales. I have a vague recollection of stripping down to my boxers in a Carmarthenshire pub, while a local farmer did something similar. Please, let me finish...He reckoned Welsh farmers had better physiques than Canadian loggers, so I just had to prove him wrong. It was the Llandovery boys who introduced me to the power shandy, a quart of beer in a vodka ice botth, and smash it back. For my part, I bequeathed them Cudmore's logger lager top - a double vodka in a bottle of bud, and obviously down in one.

And then there was the incident with the potato gun. I have to confess I'd forgotten about my spud gun, until the Llandovery party came to Clermont in 2016. The memories came flooding back, so much so that when I signed for Oyonnax in the summer of 2016 I resurrected the potato gun during a week of team bonding. Still got it!

I have Barry Davies, the Wales and Scarlets full-back, to thank for the potato gun. Barry had some yap on him and one day at training, as we ate lunch, he launched into this great spiel about how he was building a 'duchy'. What's a duchy? I asked. Turned out it was a bamboo arrow that Barry confidently asserted would fly from one end of the pitch to the other. I won't bore you with any more details.

We laid bets on how far Bazza would launch his arrow and then, with great fanfare, we trooped out onto Stradey Park as the Great Inventor appeared with his 'duchy'. OK, boys, look and learn. So we watched as the bamboo dart went 10 metres up in the air, veered off the right and ended up on the roof. Just as well Barry never embarked on a career as a military weapons manufacturer.

Trying to keep a straight face, I congratulated Barry and told him I'd try and beat his impressive benchmark with my potato gun. I said no more, but as soon as training was over I went to the hardware store and brought some pipe, a pot of glue and a saw, and spent the rest of the day building a potato gun.

We made them as kids in metalwork class at school (so at least all my years at school weren't completely wasted) so it was just a question of recalling the tricks of the trade. Satisfied with my potato gun I took it into the back garden of the terraced house I was living in. My neighbours were a couple of old priests, who liked their rugby, and luckily knew all about me. Nevertheless they were a little puzzled as I pushed a potato down this pipe and then gave a squirt of butane gas into the air chamber. 'Boom!' The potato shot out of the pipe and disappeared into the distance. A window opened above my head and one of the priests leaned out: "Jamie," he said, in his best confessional manner. "You're a bloody terrorist!"

The next day I told the boys there would be demonstration of my potato gun at lunchtime. The tension rose throughout the morning. Barry Davies was heaping the psychological pressure on me, but I was quietly confident the potato gun wouldn't let me down. We assembled in the parking lot and I asked Phil John to be my assistant. I knew I could trust Phil as my number two on the gun.

Together we smashed a potato down the barrel and he gave a little spray of gas into the air chamber and then closed it up. The tension was now unbearable. Here we go, boys, I said. I pressed the trigger. Click. Nothing! Click. Nothing! Click, click, click. The boys began rubbishing me. "Go home, Cudmore, and take your Canadian crap with you!"

I stayed calm. Dredging up all my years of spud gun experience - and knowing there was Canadian honour at stake - I figured we'd put in too much gas. I opened up the chamber, blew away the gas, and this time put in just a small squirt. Don't let me down, I muttered, as I pressed the trigger. The detonation echoed around the hallowed ground of Stradey Park and a potato arced through the air with the same grace as a Stephen Jones touchfinder. The potato landed 200 metres away and the humiliation of Barry Davies was complete.

Word of the potato gun soon spread to Llandovery and I was asked to give a demonstration one Saturday afternoon after a game. There were some youth players at the clubhouse and one in particular, displaying the cynicism of youth, challenged me to him him. I couldn't let such a challenge pass.

We stood under the posts and I was tasked with hitting him before he reached the far posts. Off he went, galloping down the pitch, and I lined up him in my sights. I never thought in a million years I could get him, so I just shot nonchalantly from the hip. The potato shot out of the gun and the next instant this young dude is prostrate on the halfway line. For a few moments everyone stared in horror at this motionless figure. Oh my God. I could see the headlines - "Cudmore Back behind Bars after Potato Slaying". At that moment the kid rose groggily to his feet, rubbing his neck as he walked unsteadily back to the clubhouse., He wasn't laughing, but everyone else in the club found the purple potato-sized bruise on his neck hilarious.

Llandovery was an outstanding experience, from a personal and team viewpoint. The 'country boys' smashed a lot of bigger clubs and we finished the 2002-03 season third in the league. I won 17 of the 23 matches I played for the club and the regular games, combined with my daily training at the Scarlets, really furthered my rugby education. I was now conscious of what was required as a professional player and I had hoped I might get another deal with the Scarlets. But it wasn't to be. I was released in the summer of 2003. It was disappointing, but understandable. It was at a time when the Welsh Rugby Union were introducing central contracts and clubs were looking to sign marquee players, not a young forward from Canada. I had an offer from Bridgend but I decided to look around, and anyway, my preoccupation in the summer of 2003 was earning a call-up to Canada's World Cup squad.

Chapter Eight

If it wasn't a challenge enough to combine my Scarlets and Llandovery commitments in 2002, I also had to fit in a couple of Test matches for Canada. The first was against Wales at the Millennium Stade on November 16. Seven days earlier I'd been playing for Llandovery against Newbridge in front of a few hundred spectators, and now I was sitting on the bench surrounded by 30,000 raucous Welsh fans.

It was a good performance from Canada and we gave Wales a run for their money, losing 32-21 against an experienced Welsh XV, most of whom would be the backbone of their side that reached the World Cup quarter-final the following year. Not long into the second-half Jared **Barker reduced the Welsh lead to 22-18 with his sixth penalty but ultimately it was the boot of one of my Scarlets' teammates, Stephen J**ones, that got Wales home with a haul of 22 points. But the day belonged to another Scarlet - Scott Quinnell. That Test was the last of his 52 appearances for Wales and he received a standing ovation from the players and fans at the end of the match. I came on for the last 16 minutes, replacing Phil Murphy in the back-row, and it was all a blur, to be honest. It was the first time I'd played in a huge stadium and in my first two Tests, against the States and Chile, there had been no more than 4,000 fans.

The intensity only increased the following week, however, when we crossed the Channel to play France at the Stade de France. Les Bleus had won the Grand Slam a few months earlier, hammering Ireland 44-5 along the way, so I knew I was in for the most physical match of my life. The whole experience was pretty overwhelming. I remember the police escort to the stadium, looking out of the window as the police motorcyclists slapped cars with their white gloves to get them out of the way. This was the big-time, my first experience of the pressure of international rugby. In the hotel in the days before the game you live, eat and breathe rugby. It's on the TV, in the newspapers, it's the only topic of conversation at the dinner table.

I was on the bench again, which gave me the ringside view of some of the world-class talent on show. The French back row that evening was Serge Betsen, Imanol **Harinordoquy** and Olivier Magne, one of their greatest combinations of all-time. At scrum-half they had Fabien Galthie, in the centre Thomas Castaignede and at hooker Raphael Ibanez. In the second-row they had a couple of monsters in Fabien Pelous and Olivier Brouzet, whose experience was as vast as their physiques. I would come up a few times against Pelous in the years to come and he's one of the best I've played against. France have never had the same aura of intimidation about them since Pelous retired after the 2007 World Cup. He was the last - possibly ever - of those French second-rows who was not only a great technician but also a fearsome warrior, who wasn't afraid to take matters into his own hands if things got a bit tasty. Perhaps it's no coincidence that France have steadily declined in the decade since he Ibanez, Betsen and Christian Califano all retired. Hard men, each and every one.

There were 50,000 people in the Stade de France and they'd come to see Canada destroyed. It didn't quite work out that way, at least not in the first-half. France turned round with a 13-0 lead thanks to a converted try from wing David Bory and a couple of penalties from fly-half Gerard Merceron. In the second-half (I came on again for the last 15 minuets) France pulled clear. They were just too fit for us. The final score of 35-3 wasn't a humiliation but nonetheless it illustrated the gulf in the professional era between the top nations and the tier two sides. Al Charron, who captained the side in the Stade de France, had been a member of the Canada team that came so close to causing a huge upset against France in the quarter-final of the 1991 World Cup. The French squeezed home 19-13 that day, one of the proudest in the history of Canadian rugby, but since the sport had turned professional four years later, Canada and the other 'smaller' rugby-playing nations had seen the tier one nations disappear into the distance thanks to their superior resources.

Not that the IRB and tier one countries didn't try and help. In the summer of 2003 the Churchill Cup was launched with the aim of exposing Canada and the USA to more regular top-grade competition against the major powers. Over the years teams from Ireland, Scotland, Italy, New Zealand and Argentina have competed but in its inaugural season the Churchill Cup featured England A, Canada and the USA. We played England first, losing 43-7 in Vancouver. Four days later we played the USA. Even by normal standards, this was a fiery encounter. There were four yellow cards - three for us, one for the States - and the States won 16-11. But we were robbed. Just ask anyone who was in the beer garden at the Thunderbird Stadium! They saw what happened. As the clock was ticking down I drove through a maul and reached out to plunk the ball over the try-line. A big cheer went up from the beer garden. But **in the split second after I had grounded the ball their scrum-half kicked it out of my hands. The unsighted ref gave a knock on. Everyone in the beer garden went crazy. So did I. I scrambled to my feet, ripped off my headgear and told the ref what I thought of his decision. The result? A yellow card and a real fear on my part that I'd jeopardized my chances of selection for the World Cup squad.**

But when Dave Clark announced the 30-man squad in August I was in. So were Al Charron and David Lougheed, who would both be heading to their fourth World Cup. I was in awe of such an achievement; playing in one was a thrill, imagine playing in four. At the time Canada were ranked 12th in the world and we were grouped with Wales, ranked ninth, Italy, 11th, and New Zealand, the number two seeds. The only team below us in the rankings was Tonga, so that was the match we targeted above all others. When Clarkie announced the squad he said it is "the best prepared, best organized and fittest ever to leave Canada". He was right, and he was also correct in saying that our aim was to reach the quarter-final.

We believed we could do that. Beating the All Blacks was never really a realistic goal, but we'd run Wales close in Cardiff nine months earlier and we fancied our chances against Italy, whose only victory in the 2003 Six Nations was a 30-22 win over the Welsh in Rome.

As it turned out we managed to beat only Tonga. Our first game was against Wales in Melbourne and we were beaten 41-10. Five days we lost 68-6 to New Zealand, which at least wasn't as bad as the 70-7 hammering they'd dished out to the Italians. But four days after encountering the All Black machine we had to play Italy. It was our third match in nine days, each one against a tier one side. The Italians had enjoyed an extra two days' rest after beating Tonga. Who knows if the outcome would have been different if the scheduling hadn't been so crazy. As it was, we lost 19-14, with Sergio Parisse getting Italy's only try. To further underline the stupidity

of the scheduling we than had eight days until our final pool match against Tonga. So three matches in nine days and then eight days off. In contrast, New Zealand's rest periods between pool games was six days, seven days and nine days.

The fixture schedule has continued to be a cause for complaint for tier two sides in every subsequent World Cup. The former Samoan lock Daniel Leo forcefully raised the issue of scheduling during the 2015 World Cup and I agree with what he said. Tier one sides receive preferential treatment at World Cups. Definitely, and yet it doesn't make sense because Tier two sides have 20 odd guys in the squad, who are at the required level, and the rest who are semi-pro or playing for smaller clubs. Yet every player in the Tier One squads is fully pro and playing for one of the big clubs, and there's no drop in quality among them. These nations can cope with shorter turnarounds between matches in a World Cup, but instead it's the tier two sides with smaller resources who get smaller rest periods because it suits the broadcasters to have the big boys playing at the weekend.

There was an improvement in the 2015 World Cup scheduling, which was long overdue, and I hope it continues in Japan in 2019. Because frankly the treatment meted out to Tier Two sides in the past has been shameful.

Take the 2007 World Cup in France. Canada had nine days between the Fiji and Japan matches, then four days between playing Japan and taking on Australia. Whereas if you look at England, New Zealand and Australia in the 2007 World Cup, they always had at least six days rest between pool matches.

That's the minimum amount of recovery time a player requires. Rugby World Cups are among the most physically demanding of any sporting event. Even at my first in 2003 - in which I started the games against New Zealand, Italy and Tonga - it took two days before I felt my body was anything like back to normal. And I was 25 then. The first day after a game the bumps and bruises are raw but the muscle soreness is at its worst 48 hours after the game. Imagine then having to play another Test match two days after that. You're back training, but still pretty beat up, and all you can do is work through any injuries or knocks. This is the point where I must salute all the Canadian medical staff who've tended to me over the years. I've been fortunate enough to work with some of the best around. Canada may be a small nation in rugby-playing terms but in sports medicine we're up there with the best and it's been my privilege to have the benefit of their knowledge and expertise.

With eight days' rest between the Italy match and our final group game of the 2003 World Cup against Tonga we were fully prepared. It was a significant match for Canadian rugby: not only the 50th cap for Mike James but also the last appearances in a red shirt for Bob Ross and Al Charron. Unfortunately one of the great servants of Canadian rugby was in no fit state to savour our 24-7 victory. Ten minutes from time Al was on the receiving end of a wild tackle from Tongan fly-half Pierre Hola. Big Al is one of the hardest men I've ever played with or against on a rugby field but Hola's hit would have felled a rhinoceros. He might have been a fly-half but he weighed in at 100kg. He made no attempt to legitimately tackle Al, he basically shoulder-charged his head. Al collapsed unconscious to the ground, blood gushing from his mouth. The end of a magnificent 13-year Test career. How Hola stayed on the field was a mystery. He should have been, at the very least, sent to the sin bin, but referee Alain Rolland said it wasn't a dangerous tackle. As Dave Clark said afterwards: "He was hit very hard and I think he's going to need about 740,000 stitches in his mouth."

Al wasn't the only Canadian on the receiving end of the Tongan's borderline physicality. Marco di Girolamo also departed with blood streaming from his face after getting a boot in his face and James Pritchard was shoulder-charged by David Palu for which he received a yellow card.

But we kept our discipline to pull clear in the second-half and it was fitting that Bobby Ross was instrumental in steering us to victory. Bob made his Canadian debut in 1989 against Ireland and ended it fourteen years and 58 caps later by landing four penalties. That was my first match against one of the Pacific Island nations and I wouldn't describe it as a step-up in intensity from what had gone before. There are no soft matches in the World Cup and we'd just come through encounters Wales and New Zealand. Everyone hits hard in the Test arena, it's just the Tongans tend to hit a little higher than most.

Once incident I'd like to mention from the 2003 World Cup concerns Brad Thorn, my opposite number when we played New Zealand in Melbourne. After the match I went into the All Blacks' dressing room to swap jerseys with Brad. Like me, he was making his way in international rugby, having made his All Black debut just a few months' earlier, but when I suggested a swap he turned me down. He'd already pledged to give the jersey to a charity. No problem. We exchanged a friendly few words and that was that, I forgot all about it. Eight years later Canada and New Zealand met again at the World Cup, this time in Wellington. There was no official reception after the match, there wasn't time for one, so instead we all went into the All Black dressing room with a couple of crates of beer. Brad was away doing press interviews but Ali Williams handed me Brad's jersey and said he hadn't forgotten about eight years earlier, and he was just sorry he wasn't able to trade personally. So I finally got my hands on his New Zealand jersey and I was fortunate to play against Brad - one of the best I've encountered - a few more times in the following seasons when he signed for Leinster.

When I arrived in Australia for the 2003 World Cup I was still without a club. I'd had a few offers but the tournament, and the training camp going into it, had allowed me time to consider my options. One of those options was a move to France to play for Grenoble, which had come about thanks to Mike James. He had been playing in France for a number of years, first with Perpignan and then Stade Francais, and he put me in touch with his agent. Soon I was speaking to Willy Taofifénua, who had spent a decade playing for Grenoble before becoming their coach and then their manager.

I'd done a bit of research on the club, and the city, which is in the shadow of the Alps, and everything looked good. When I wasn't playing rugby they would be plenty of opportunities to indulge my love of outdoor sports: some skiing, bit of hunting, perhaps even some rafting in the summer. It would just like being back in Vancouver, only on a bigger salary.

Chapter Nine

When I think back to my time at Grenoble it feels like another era, which I guess in a way it was. Compared to the minutely-programmed way of life for the modern professional player, the two seasons I spent at Grenoble were incredibly unsupervised. We had regular training, of course, but what we didn't have was anywhere near the same levels of sophistication in terms of medicine, nutrition, video analysis and fitness. Back in the day, video analysis consisted of the squad watching a replay of the match with the coach stopping the tape at certain points with the remote control. Something would usually go wrong: the batteries might run out in the remote control or the coach accidentally presses the fast-forward button instead of the pause. Those of us old enough can remember what it was like in the olden days.

By the time I left Clermont in 2016 we could have blood tests if we felt sick or low on energy; drones filmed training sessions to give the coaching staff a different perspective; we used GPS (Global Positioning System), which recorded data on players' running distances allowing coaches to reduce the workload in training to have us in better shape for the weekend. All matches were available on bluetooth with the games coded, so if you wanted to look at any opponent in the Top 14 or Champions Cup it was instantly available. These were further broken down into a database of every aspect of the match: defence, set-piece, attacking moves,etc. You just clicked and watched.

There was none of that at Grenoble in 2003. But what there was was a lot of was skiing. Come on, the Alps were on my doorstep, what the hell was I supposed to do?! My regular skiing buddies were Rickus Lubbe, Daniel Browne and Julien Puricelli. Whenever we had a chunk of spare time we would head into the mountains for some skiing followed by a raclette and a few beers. I know some players have it written into their contracts that they must not participate in extreme sports or any dangerous activity. Not me. And when I was skiing at Grenoble I took a lot of risks on the slopes.

The life of a professional player was so much different then. You trained as a squad for a couple of hours in the morning, did an hour's weights, and then had the rest of the day off. Perfect for a young, single guy with a set of skis.

I'm going to sound a bit like one of those old bastards now, the 'In my day' brigade, but hell, who cares! When I turned pro in 2002 there was no social media, no facebook, snapchat or twitter. Some of the boys spent too much time on video games (never my thing, my fingers are too fat) but we made our own entertainment without tap, tap, tapping away on our i-phones. Sure, I use social media now, but I'm not addicted to it, and more importantly, I still place more value on face to face conversations.

In recent seasons squad bonding sessions have become less and less sociable. You go to a restaurant with the boys and half of them spend the whole night on their phones. There's less social interaction and that's down - ironic, given the name - to social media. The bottom line is it makes getting to know your teammates harder. When I joined Oyonnax we had a team outing on the final day of our block of summer training, and as we entered the restaurant there was a bucket into which we all had to drop our phones. One or two of the boys grumbled at first, but it turned into a great evening and the grumblers soon admitted they enjoyed a few hours away from their phones. So much of the time we don't need to be checking twitter or facebook, we do it by force of habit.

The other negative impact of social media is the erosion of trust between player and public. Nowadays there's a saying 'if there's no picture, I don't believe you', so everybody's got to have a photo or a snapchat or a video. A decade ago I'd never heard of a selfie, nowadays it's the first word on a lot of supporters' lips. Most of the time I'm only too happy to pose with the fans because overall my experience of French rugby fans is that they're pretty respectful of my privacy. If I'm in a restaurant with my family they won't come marching up to the table demanding a selfie.

But at the back of the mind there's always a nagging question - is this person going to try and stitch me up because he or she doesn't like me or my team? These days you have to be careful of who you are with and who is around you, particularly in a bar or restaurant, when you may have had a beer or a glass of wine, and your guard is slightly down. It's much easier to be photographed in a compromising situation, or what looks to be a compromising situation. It could be perfectly innocent but uploaded on twitter with a suitably sly comment and the truth becomes distorted. Any photo I publish on social media I'm conscious that I'm representing my club, my sponsors and myself, and as a pro athlete it's not good for my image if I have a beer in one hand. These days an image can be formed of someone with just one fleeting photo, and if you aren't careful then one or two ill-advised photos could convey totally the wrong image and contrary to the one you want to cultivate. It takes a lot of work to keep control of it and undoubtedly social media has broken some of the trust between players and fans.

I feel for the young players today. I look back to what I was like at 18 and 19 and I'm very relieved social media is a recent invention. No question, I would have run into trouble. What am I saying? I have run into trouble on social media and I'm in my late 30s. I mean, I would have run into more trouble!

Most young professional players today receive training in how to handle the traditional media and also how to use social media. It's important they're aware of the perils because once you post a photo it's out there and there's no getting it back.

If asked I'm happy to dole out advice to younger players, not just on social media but life in general. I've got quite a bit of life experience under my belt so if any of it can be useful, then great.

Broadening this subject of young professionals today, another difference between their generation and mine is their competence as human beings. The overwhelming majority of professional players in their twenties have never worked in a 'real job', and you see it in the way they go about certain actions and tasks. These boys are in for a hell of a wake-up call when they go out into the real world because they are not used to making decisions for themselves.

As a professional player so much is done for you, so much is planned. Practically every waking minute of your life is organised by someone else. You've got to be at X, Y and Z at a certain hour. When that is all you've known for 10 or 15 years it's a hell of a shock to wake up one day as an ex-rugby player. Suddenly there is no weekly schedule stuck on the fridge door. It's you making the decisions. It's no surprise that an increasing number of players find themselves lost when they retire, unable to adjust to life outside the rigid framework of professional rugby.

Additionally, ex-players no longer have the adulation from the fans. Don't let anyone tell they don't like being recognised around town for what they do: we all do. But you're quickly forgotten once you're no longer in the spotlight. There are new heroes to worship, new selfies to take, and a lot of guys find it a severe blow to their self-esteem when their career is over and their status is dramatically reduced.

So it's important that players plan for the future even when their rugby careers are at their peak. A serious injury could bring their world crashing down and it's vital to have a safety net. The impress I have is that clubs are much better at working with their players to prepare for their lives outside rugby. I can only speak intimately of Clermont but they were very good at offering either help, services or education, to players.

*

When I arrived at Grenoble after the 2003 World Cup everything was going well. The previous season the club had finished fourth in its pool - these were the days when the French championship comprised 16 clubs split into two pools with the top four in each pool advancing to a play-off - and there was no indication of the trouble that lay ahead. Grenoble had been promoted from the ProD2 in May 2002 and its ambition was to consolidate its place in the elite of French rugby. The coaches were Jacques Delmas and Pierre Trémouille, and the squad was a mix of foreign guys and talented French players.

I was impressed with Delmas. I found him an excellent coach and he **improved my running lines and gave me a bit of French flair to my game. Unfortunately in recent years I appear to have mislaid it. Jacques was complemented by Pierre Tremouille, the backs' coach, who knew his stuff and had the respect of the players. But the pair paid the price for a poor season and were fired by Grenoble in June 2004. It hadn't been that bad; we'd finished second bottom in the pool but we hadn't disgraced ourselves. We simply weren't good enough to compete with the likes of Toulouse, Biarritz and Perpignan, who at the time were three of the powerhouses of French rugby.**

Thirteen years later all three are no longer the force they were. Toulouse are still in the Top 14, though their days as the dominant European club are long gone, while Biarritz and Perpignan were relegated to the ProD2 in 2014 and have recently experienced financial problems.

That's exactly what happened to Grenoble in my second season. In a word, everything went tits up that year and by early 2005 Grenoble resembled a French farce. It was too early in my career to understand the politics and drama of French rugby, though to be honest I still don't. A lot of clubs are a law unto themselves and often the chaos percolates from the president. That was the case at Grenoble where Alain Etievent eventually ended up in court charged with financial irregularity stemming from his time as president. He'd arrived in September 2001, a few months after the club had been relegated to the ProD2 after 15 years in the top flight, and he was faced with a €1.5m financial hole. Within a season Etievent had transformed the fortunes of the club and the players had done the business on the field, getting Grenoble back to the Top 16.

Everything looked rosy, and the disappointment of losing Delmas and Tremouille was offset by the appointment as head coach of Dean Richards. 'Deano' was a legend in the game, a brilliant No8 for England the Lions in the late 1980s and early 1990s, who then went on to forge a successful career as coach of Leicester. He'd guided the Tigers to four successive English league titles and also back-to-back Heineken Cup crowns in 2001 and 2002. He'd left Leicester at the start of February 2004 after 18 months without a trophy, but that hardly dimmed his reputation and I was certainly excited at the prospect of working under him.

Deano made an instant impression with his ability to speak French and his willingness to embrace the differences in culture between Grenoble and Leicester, the club he'd been with in one capacity or another for 23 years. Dean did his best to organise a good squad with tough forwards, and backs who wanted to play some good rugby. But Dean, in how he approached the job, was more a manager than a coach, but Grenoble wanted him only as a coach. That was one problem; the other was the growing antagonism between the French players and the foreign ones. It had been there since the start of the season but when we began to lose some matches the tensions grew. It was a shame because we fought hard in most matches. Our only two thrashings were the 36-3 defeat away at Toulouse and the 47-7 hammering at Biarritz; other than that we were competitive in most matches but defeat breeds despondency, and in Grenoble's case, disunity.

Dean appointed me captain in an attempt to bring the two warring factions together. By now I could speak a bit of French and I was one of the few foreigners who had the respect of the French boys. I tried my utmost to heal the differences but some guys really dug in their heels and didn't want to compromise. As the season wore on some players stopped talking to each other, although in truth there hadn't been a great deal of dialogue at the best of times because most of the foreign guys didn't make an effort to talk French. This created resentment among the French, and the situation degenerated to the point where players' would go on the piss between matches and not carry themselves like professional sportsmen.

And then the financial problems emerged. Looking back on what happened at Grenoble I still find it scarcely believable that a club that was so well supported by fans, that had a stadium funded by the city council and that had recruited a strong squad with a top coach, could then go and screw it all up. Completely ridiculous. When the dust settled on Grenoble's 2004-05 season Dean Richards and Alain Etievent had gone and the club was demoted two divisions to Federale One because of financial impropriety. That wasn't all. I'd also left. My two seasons at Grenoble had been interesting, to say the least. Initial enjoyment had turned to exasperation and I knew midway through the second season that I had to escape. There were rumours already circulating that the D.N.A.C.G (Direction Nationale d'Aide et de Contrôle de Gestion), the financial regulators who manage professional rugby, were scrutinising the accounts of Grenoble and I thought it wise to start shopping around. As luck would have it, I soon received an approach from Clermont, and at their invitation I went to have a look round the Stade Marcel Michelin. I liked what I saw and in the early summer of 2005 I signed for Les Januards.

Chapter Ten

When I arrived at Clermont it was to find that **Olivier Saïsset was no longer coach. He'd been the man who had enticed me to the club but he was now gone, replaced by Philippe Agostini at the start of the 2005-06 season. Philippe, who was assisted by Jean-Pierre Laparra, was OK but** he was really a puppet for Jean-Marc Lhermet, the club's sporting director. More about Lhermet later.

It was too bad that Agostini wasn't really up to the job because we had a hell of a squad. Predominantly French - this was before the era of foreign players flooding the Top 14 - there were a handful of outsiders. South African wing Breyton Paulse was one, former All Black loose forward Sam Broomhall another and I also got the chance to hook up with an old Scarlets' buddy of mine, Wales fly-half Stephen Jones, who was in the second year of a two-season stint at the club. It was good to see a familiar face when I walked into the dressing room for the first time and Steve was awesome in helping me find my feet.

So we had the talent but what Agostini never managed to instil into the squad was 'rigueur'. There was still back then this attitude almost unique in world rugby to France of not really caring about away matches. An example in my first season at Clermont was when we slaughtered Toulon 65-0 at home and then lost the following week to Narbonne, one of the weaker teams in the league (the French championship was reorganised for the start of the 2005-06 season into its current format of 14 clubs in one league).

Attitudes were not good enough and there was no real steel in the club. This came from the top down. Philippe had come from the Clermont Under-21 set up and was used to coaching kids. He wasn't hard enough on us, whether because he was intimidated or because he just didn't know how to get the best of out professional players.

Clermont finished the 2005-06 season in eighth position, outside the play-offs and nearly thirty points behind first placed Perpignan. Fortunately changes were made that summer. The president of the club was Rene Fontes, and Jacques Pineau was the vice-president.

They worked well as a team and Rene in particular was a class act. He's a very personable guy with a successful track record in the business world and he ran the club really well. I never really regarded the Michelin crowd that highly, as I'll explain later, but Rene was one of the few from the company who was switched on. When he left Clermont in 2013 the club lost something. In my opinion his successor, **Éric de Cromières, isn't a good figurehead. He doesn't project the same positive image as Rene did. Rene was particularly effective at** dealing with sponsors and making them feel appreciated.

But the most significant achievement of Rene's time as president was his appointment as head coach of Vern Cotter in the summer of 2006. Vern has become a good friend of mine so I admit I write these words with a touch of partiality but his arrival at Clermont transformed the club.

It was a real eye-opener for a lot of boys when he walked into the dressing room. Life had been pretty relaxed life under Agostini, well, that soon changed. It didn't take Vern long to figure out that while the squad had talent there was little in the way of work ethic and attention to detail. He soon began drilling a work ethic into us.

Vern's not much of a shouter, though he will when it's needed. But he speaks his mind and doesn't let people push around him. He has his way of doing things and expects players to fall in line. He could be ruthless with those who didn't strive to reach the standards he set, but that was because he couldn't understand any player - who obviously had talent - who wasn't prepared to fulfil their potential by working hard.

In that first season Vern spoke at length to each player individually, outlining what he saw as their strengths and weaknesses, and the areas that they particularly needed to work on. My main weakness? Got it in one. I knew that I had to improve discipline to be a regular part of squad so did a lot of work on playing on an edge but without going over the line between aggression and illegality.

Since establishing myself in the Canada XV in the 2003 World Cup I'd worked hard to tighten my discipline. I kept my nose clean in the World Cup and in my first season at Grenoble I'd received one yellow and one red card. I wobbled from the

straight and narrow in my second season, receiving eight yellow cards. Considering I played 21 matches that season it was a poor disciplinary record and one I had to improve.

It was marginally better in my first season at Clermont. I was sent to the sin-bin three times and red-carded once. That was unfair, though. No, honest! I was sent off for swearing at the referee in a game against Montpellier. But I hadn't sworn at the ref. He'd shown me a yellow for a reckless challenge and when the captain told me, I exclaimed: 'You've got to be fucking kidding!' The ref heard the 'fucking' and not having a good grasp of English thought it was directed at him. It wasn't but off I went although the red card was later overturned on appeal.

May I just take a moment to point out that was only the second of four red cards in my career. Considering I'm in my 15th season of professional rugby that's not so bad. Yellow is more my colour - I believe at the last count I had passed the 30 mark in French rugby - but that still only works out at two a season. May I also, your honour, in my defence state that most of my time in the sin bin has been the result of reckless and not malicious challenges. I've never set out to damage an opponent; like I said I play the game on the very edge and a few times I've gone over the edge and been rightly punished.

With Vern at the club Clermont began to fulfil its potential. We moved from being a mid-table club to a title contender, and we also reproduced our league form in the European Challenge Cup. It might have been the little brother to the Heineken Cup but Vern wanted to win it as a statement of intent. The club had won it once before, in 1999, but that feat was a little diluted by the fact the English clubs had boycotted the competition that year because of political squabbling.

But the English clubs were there in 2006-07 and one of them, Bath, were our opponents in the final. The match was in England, at the Stoop Memorial ground, home to Harlequins and situated just across the road from Twickenham. Appearing in the Challenge Cup final was the pinnacle of my club career to that date. When I'd started out playing rugby I had watched some of the European matches on TV, never imagining that a few years later I would be playing in a final.

It was a tight first 40, and we trailed 6-3 at the turnaround, but we dominated the second period, scoring 19 unanswered points to eventual run out 22-16 winners. We had a big pack with the likes of myself, **Elvis Vermeulen, Thibaut Privat and Mario Ledesma, while out wide we had guys with gas such as Julien Malzieu and Aurelien Rougerie.** Bath were playing catch-up rugby in the second half and our victory was the reward for the work we'd put in under Vern.

The Challenge Cup win was one of the final acts in the careers of a couple of old timers at Clermont - Michael Dieude and Tony Marsh. Dieude was a hell of a flanker, one of those tall, rangy No7s, who was good in the line-out and a real force around the field. I was especially sorry to see Tony Marsh leave the club. We'd become good friends in the two years we played together and he more than anyone had helped me settle in at the club and in the town. Tony also taught me more about professionalism and what was required of a player on and off the field. Tony is a tough character. He'd come through a cancer battle a few years earlier, and the way he fought back to full fitness epitomised his focus and commitment. Tony wasn't much of a rugby name when he arrived from his native New Zealand in France in 1998 but by the time he left Clermont he was one of the best centres around with 21 France caps to his name.

But before Tony could hang up his boots he and the rest of the squad had to finish the Top 14 campaign. We were third at the end of the regular season, and that meant a semi-final in Marseille against Toulouse, who finished second behind Stade Francais.

I had been struggling with a groin problem in the lead-up to the semi-final and although I was passed fit I took the field strapped from my mid-section all the way down to my knee. I had nowhere near full mobility and I lasted about 30 minutes before I was replaced by Lois Jacquet. But a try in each half from Tony Marsh and Aurelien Rougerie saw Clermont reach their first Championship final since 2001. Overall, it was our eighth appearance in the final, stretching back to 1936, and yet we'd lost them all. If we were to break that miserable sequence we'd have to beat Stade Francais. They had been the most consistent team in the championship and boasted three members of the Argentine team that a few months later would reach the semi-final of the World Cup - Juan Martín Hernández, Agustín Pichot and Rodrigo Roncero. Also in their pack was my old Canada buddy, Mike James, along with the only player I've ever truly detested - **Rémy Martin. The guy's a cock-sucker. I've had some battles over the years, notably with Gregory le Corvec, the Perpignan flanker. But Greg's a great guy. Sure, we smashed each other a couple of times in 2010, but we get on fine off the field. Martin is different. He's the only player I've received multiple bad gestures from. He's put his fingers in my eyes, he's fish-hooked me from behind, he's hit me with some cheap shots. He's one of those guys who liked to act the big, tough man but when the shit hit the fan he'd be the first hiding behind his scrum-half. It's a shame because he was a good player, and he could have been France's No7 for years, but he was just too stupid. I've done some dumb things in my time but you have to adapt, you have to change your game. You can't always play the big brute but Martin didn't understand that. Clermont dominated the first half. The pack had a hell of a first forty minutes and blew the Stade scrum off the pack. We bossed the line-outs and I remember stealing one Stade ball from which Pierre Mignoni fed Tony Marsh, who made good ground towards their 22, allowing Anthony Floch the opportunity to drop a goal. A few minutes later I nicked another Stade line-out and this time we were awarded a penalty that James landed.**

Early in the second-half we were leading 12-0 and 71 years of misery looked set to end. But within the space of four minutes both me and Thibaut Privat left the field. The groin problem that had forced me off in the semi-final flared up and it was a massive disappointment to limp off six minutes into the second-half. But at least I did so pretty confident we were on our way to victory.

What happened in the final half hour had more to do with Clermont's attitude than the departure of me and Thibaut. We'd been so dominant we thought the game was won. We eased off and stopped playing with the controlled ferocity of the first 50 minutes. Stade Francais had some world-class players and they sensed straight away that our intensity was waning. Pichot and Hernandez began asserting their influence and they clawed their way back into the match, ultimately snatching victory in the dying minutes when **Radike**

Samo scored in the corner. It was a devastating defeat for everyone at the club. The game had been there for the taking but once again we'd let it slip through our fingers. Looking back on the match one moment sticks in my mind as being pivotal. About five minutes before half-time we were awarded a penalty when, despite our superiority, all we had to show were three points. I believe we should have kicked into the corner and gone for the try because we were so dominant up front. But we went for the safe option and kicked a penalty to extend our lead to 6-0. It's one of those decisions that you make in the heat of the moment. Personally I wanted to go for the line-out because I was confident we could win it and then drive over for the try. That would have opened up a healthy lead and dealt a big psychological blow to Stade. Rougerie was the captain and it was his call to go for the posts. You can understand why. Finals are usually tight affairs with only a few points separating triumph from disaster so if points are on offer, take them. But Rougerie was captaining from the wing and I don't believe that's where you want your skipper to be; he needs to be in the heart of action, preferably in the back-row or at half-back. There you have a much better feel for the game. You can hear its heartbeat and also get a sense of how the ref is seeing the match. That is impossible if you're out on the wing. If the captain in the 2007 final had been in the pack he would have known how dominant we were and we would probably have kicked for the corner and scored from the line-out.

The only solace for me from that 2007 defeat was that Mike James ended his career on a high. he retired at the end of the season and he deserved to go out a winner after an outstanding career,

Chapter Eleven

The Republic Bar is just off George Street in St John's, Newfoundland. It is, or at least it was on 12 August 2006, owned by some local rugby guys, so it was the obvious place to celebrate our crushing victory over the USA. We had humped the Americans 56-7, which remains a record winning margin in matches between the two nations. It was one of those matches when everything clicked and we gave the 5,000 fans a treat. Up front our set-piece was rock solid and Rod Snow, in particular, made some big carries. I had a couple of good charges myself, one after just seven minutes when our prop Kevin Tkachuk took a quick tap penalty. I took a pop pass and made some good ground before offloading to David Spicer and he in turn brushed aside a couple of tacklers to give fullback Mike Pyke the pass that led to the try.

As we softened up the Eagles in the pack, we began to wreak out wide with wing James Pritchard scoring a hat-trick of tries and ending the day with an incredible

36 points, thanks to nine shots at goal.

The win was not only our biggest over our neighbours but it secured our qualification for the 2007 World Cup. It was time to party, right? So we did.

Test match rugby rarely comes to St John's - in fact that Test is the only international I've played in Newfoundland - with Vancouver, Calgary and Toronto seeing most of the action. And being a west coast boy I didn't know St John's. I was there to have a good time before flying back to France the next day to begin pre-season training with Clermont.

It wasn't long before the beers were flowing and at one point in the evening I was standing on the bar pretending to be a pirate. I've got a vague recollection of waving a plastic sword at the bartender and demanding a flagon of foaming ale otherwise I'd make him walk the plank. Something like that. Then I remember glancing round and seeing this big table of girls, and among them this tall beautiful blonde.

Despite growing up in a pretty masculine environment I've never been socially awkward in front of the opposite sex. Even as an 11, 12 year old, when a lot of boys go bright red at the sight of a girl, I was at ease in their company. Not in a flirtatious way, just chatting to them without any self-consciousness. The girls I grew up with Squamish matched the boys in everything we did. If a group of boys went fishing so the girls would come; if we went snowboarding they'd join us, same for skiing, messing about in the river, whatever. I've never had any time for sexism or sexists.

It's fantastic to see the huge development and growth in women's rugby over the last few years, and I have to give a special mention to the Canadian women's Sevens squad, who won a bronze medal at the 2016 Olympics. What an awesome achievement. The squad is coached by an old buddy of mine, John Tait, who I played with a few times for Canada. By a stroke of good fortune they played in a tournament in Clermont a couple of months before flying out to Rio for the Olympics. I took my daughter, Maelle, to meet some of the players and watch them in action. Rugby is a sport for all shapes and sizes and sexes, and I want Maelle to know that if she wants to play rugby she can. If she doesn't enjoy it, that's fine. But it's important for her to understand from an early age that there are no barriers in sport because of your sex.

But back to the bar and my piracy. Having spotted this statuesque blonde I leapt from the bar and in my best swashbuckling manner introduced myself. Her name was Jennifer and it was my very, very lucky day that she was in the bar. Luck, and the persistence of her old man, Ken.

Jennifer was a native of Newfoundland but in 2006 she was living in Ottawa working in the fashion industry. On the Friday before the match she decided at the last minute to fly home to Newfoundland to spend the weekend with her mum and dad. She wasn't feeling too well on the Saturday, she had a sore throat, but Ken had got a couple of tickets for the Canada v USA game and he wouldn't take no for an answer. So Jennifer went, met a few old friends, and to cut a long story short was in the Republic bar after the match.

We hit it off straight away. More or less. Being a pirate I made off with her purse on the end of my sword but I soon returned my booty and we spent the rest of the evening talking. She had no idea who I was, although she guessed I was a rugby player, but when the next morning she told her mum about our meeting, she mentioned my name. Cudmore! She knew that name. Katy McIntosh's book about the death of Bob was just about to be published and there had been some pre-publication articles in magazines and newspapers. Jenny's mum had read one and that's how she knew my name. Fortunately neither Jennifer or her mum judged me on that article.

I had flown back to France on the Sunday after meeting Jennifer but we'd exchanged email addresses with a promise to keep in touch. Jennifer had applied to do an MBA (The Master of Business Administration) in Melbourne having spent a year in Australia after leaving university. She wasn't offered a place in Melbourne but she was at Grenoble. That was a big surprise because it was an MBA in international management and Jennifer didn't think she had the age or experience. Grenoble thought otherwise and to my delight she was soon in France.

I met her at the airport and obviously having spent a couple of seasons in Grenoble I was able to help her settle in. There are a couple of hundred miles between

Clermont and Grenoble but whenever I had any time off I would spend it with Jennifer.

It wasn't all plain sailing. At the time I was living in an apartment block owned by Clermont. My brother, Luke, was sharing the flat with me and we had a cat called Spike. Spike was a sweetie though he did have a nasty habit of peeing indoors. So the apartment didn't smell too fragrant. And Jennifer's allergic to cats. Add to that the sweaty rugby kit and the fact the walls of the apartment were stained black from the Michelin factory smoke and it probably wasn't the first choice a guy would choose to romance his girlfriend.

A solution was found in early 2008 when Sam Broomhall returned to New Zealand. He and his wife had rented a beautiful apartment on the north side of Clermont so Jennifer and I took over the lease. Oh, I forgot to mention, by this time we were married!

I actually put a huge amount of planning into the proposal. Having got permission from Ken to ask for his daughter's hand in marriage, I ordered an engagement ring through a buddy I knew in Vancouver. I wanted a nice Canadian rock. The trickiest part was organising the actual proposal. In the summer of 2007 I returned to Canada for a World Cup training camp in Vancouver and that was quite intense with the tournament only a few weeks' away. The one window of opportunity was a couple of days off after we'd beaten a British Columbia XV in a warm-up match. I jumped on a plane and flew the nine and a half hours from Vancouver to Halifax and then on to St John's. Meanwhile the woman I hoped would be my mother-in-law was making sure her daughter didn't leave the house. Jennifer had come to Canada on vacation with Libby James, the wife of my Australian teammate at Clermont, Brock, and she was also in on the secret. Jennifer's told me subsequently that she thought both her mum and Libby were acting a little 'weird' during the day. I arrived at the house in the early evening and with a thumping heart knocked on the door. The moment Jennifer opened the door I dropped to one knee and asked her to marry me. I was pretty relived with her answer. I didn't fancy a nine and a half hour return flight to Vancouver with 'No' ringing in my ears.

We didn't have a big wedding. In fact, we sort of eloped, flying to New York to tie the knot in a very low-key ceremony. Neither of us wanted all the palava of planning a huge wedding with hundreds of guests. We loved each other and wanted to spend the rest of your lives together. That's what mattered.

So we moved into the Broomhalls' old place and that was good, but really, what we wanted was a home of our own. Trouble was we wanted somewhere with a lot of space and light, and a big deck so we could live outside during the warm months. But unless you pay upwards of €750,000 those houses are out of reach. The alternative was to build our own home. I put out some feelers in Clermont but the first plots I examined were too small. Then the **guy who was going to help with the excavation said he might have a suitable plot of land above his own property in Soulasse, a picturesque village about 25 kms south of Clermont. As soon as we saw it we knew we'd found the site of our home. Stunning views across the valley to Clermont, woods at the back for Jennifer to run, the village petanque court just up the road and within easy reach of the ski slopes. Perfect.**

I designed the house with an architect and we had a block plan that we moved around on a computer until I was satisfied. Then I bought the plans off the architect and ran with it. Luke, my brother, came over from Canada and helped with the construction work. A quick word about Luke. He's my youngest brother, and the tallest of us. Last time we got the tape measure out he was 2m04, Daniel 1m99 and I'm the runt of the litter at 1m95. Luke was a fine rugby player and won a cap for Canada in 2008 against the USA. It's a huge regret of mine that I wasn't playing that day, it would have been something special to pack down alongside Luke. We did that just once, playing for Capilanos many years ago. He was in the back-row and I got my one and only outing at fly-half. I thought I had an outstanding game with my silky skills but strangely I never received another opportunity to showcase my fly-half talent. Injuries unfortunately cut short Luke's rugby career and he's now doing well for himself in the Canadian construction industry. Daniel also played a bit in his youth - and we once turned out for the Axemen together, much to my dad's delight - but he was too good-looking for rugby. So instead he went to Hollywood

where's forged a movie career appearing in, among others, the X-Men franchise and also the Twilight Saga films. But I'm glad to say despite being a Hollywood big-shot he's never forgotten he's a Squamish boy at heart! I'm hugely proud of Luke and Dan and all they've achieved. They're my brothers and my buddies, and whenever we get together good times ensue.

I couldn't have built the house without Luke's help. It was a massive undertaking made all the more challenging by the language barrier and the different construction procedures to those I'd known in Vancouver. One of the most frustrating aspects was the readiness of the builders to down tools when it rained. In Canada you're on site whatever the weather but I lost count of the number of times the builders didn't show up in the morning because it was raining. There were a lot of battles fought on that issue.

It was all the more frustrating because not long after we started constructing the house we moved out of our spacious flat in Clermont and into a horrible little apartment fifty metres from our new place. It was a dump. One bedroom, a shitty staircase and a tiny bathroom. We envisaged being there for two months but because of the delays in building work we were there for seven. We were so desperate to get out that we moved into our home way before it was completed. But living in a half-built home was preferable to a cramped dump, particularly as Jennifer was now pregnant.

As well as building our house, we also opened at this time a nightclub called 'The Five' in the centre of Clermont. We ran that for three years, sold it, and then opened a wine bar called Vinomania, which we sold a couple of years later. We made a tidy profit on the wine bar because when we bought the property it was a defunct franchise that cost us about 300 euros. We sold it for a heavy mark-up and had a good time in the interim. It was fun dabbling in the hospitality industry but the French authorities don't make it easy to run your own business so in the end the charges and all the bureaucracy became too much to bear and we sold up.

Maelle was born in October 2010 and less than a year later she was in New Zealand watching her old man play for Canada in the World Cup. Maelle's brother,

Grayson, was born in the summer of 2012 and they can both now speak better French than their parents. They're great kids and Jennifer and I are lucky that they're so adaptable. We thought long and hard about uprooting them when my time ran out at Clermont, and one of the primary reasons why I signed a four-year deal with Oyonnax was because of the children. They're both bi-lingual but France is their home, especially Maelle who loves the country. I had offers from English clubs in early 2016 but ultimately Jennifer and I decided it would be best for the kids if we stayed in France. To make our love for France official we became French citizens in 2016. It made sense. We're proud to live in France - I've spent a quarter of my life in the country - and I want to be a part of France and at the same time give something back. Being granted citizenship is a rigorous procedure. We had to undergo all sorts of tests, testing our language and knowledge of French history. There was an interview with the police - probably the first time I've left a police station without being charged with anything - and a meeting at the prefecture. It took a year and a half from start to finish but we've know got our letter from the President welcoming us as citizens of France.

One thing I'm conscious of as a professional athlete is not pushing my kids to follow my path into sport. If as they get older Maelle and Grayson discover a talent and passion for sport then great, I'll support them all the way, but neither Jennifer nor I are the type of parents who will push them towards sport. I think back to my own experiences skiing. All I did between the ages of 12 and 16 was ski, ski, ski and I soon burned out. That wasn't my dad's fault. He encouraged me and my brothers to play sport, and always told us to do the best we can, but he never pushed me. In my case it was the coaches, who treated skiing as a job more than a sport. Slowly the fun went out of skiing because I spent all my time doing gates, always trying to get faster and always on the clock. Skiing, like all sports, should first and foremost be fun for children. Of course you need to work hard on your skills but you've got to complement the hard, tedious training with fun elements otherwise the children lose interest. And that's particularly true in today's world when there are so many other attractions competing for kids' attention.

I've done quite a bit of kids' coaching in recent years and more and more I see pushy parents, and I see the negative effect it has on their kids. On a few occasions I've come close to telling some parents to shut up and back off but it's not my place to parent other people's children. But they need to know the damage they are doing to their kids. It's the cadets age-group where you see the worst behaviour. I'm talking specifically now about Clermont. These mums and dads **think their kids are going to go on and play for ASM, be rugby superstars, and so they push and push, and shout and shout. All that does is create pressure on their children and their teammates. Just back off! These are 14 and 15 year-olds and at that age all they want to do is enjoy their rugby. It's easy to spot the children with pushy parents. They are the ones who don't react well to the pressure and their heads drop if things don't go well on the pitch.**

There's definitely an element of parents trying to live out unfulfilled dreams through their children, whether it's in France with rugby or Canadian hockey. You know, the high school sports star **who never went on to make the big-time, and so they channel their disappointment and frustration through their kids. It's sad.**

I have similar feelings towards some junior coaches I've encountered. They shout at their kids to win, win, win and stand on the sideline hollering at these 13-year-olds to smash the opposition and be aggressive. At the end of the day it's just a game and you need kids to play, and the more they play the better they are going to get. Everything needs to be based around playing games. Don't spend too much time on ruck placements,cleanouts and drills, not at that age. That stuff will come in time but first let kids play and enjoy themselves and then the base skills - which of course are important - will follow.

Chapter Twelve

Clermont were back at the Stade de France in June 2008 for the Top 14 final. We lost again. This time 26-20 to Toulouse. It was our discipline that let us down. We gave Toulouse five kickable penalty attempts and they took four of them. In contrast Brock James scored two penalties to go with the two tries we scored. I had a large hand in the first of those tries in the 20th minute. James sent through a lovely little chip kick for Marius Joubert and Aurelien Rougerie to chase. The ball took a wicked bounce, eluding everyone, except Toulouse prop Daan Human. He gathered it, and took a huge hit from me for his pains, spilling the ball over his try-line and allowing Rougerie the chance to reach out a hand for a try. I was aware of none of this. There'd been a clash of heads when I tackled Daan and I came off worst. Off I went to have a gaping hole in my head stitched and though I returned I wasn't 100%. I lasted 56 minutes and then retired.

So defeat was doubly painful that evening. It was Toulouse's 17th championship crown and Clermont's ninth defeat in the final. The wait went on. It was a bitter blow for us all, none more so than Rougerie who has been the heart and soul of Clermont since practically he made his debut as a 19-year-old in 1999. Roro is one of Aurelien's nicknames, although we used to call him 'The Little Prince', such is his standing in

Clermont. He can be a bit headstrong at times but he's **one hell of a player and a man who always showed up on the big occasion. There are some players who are touted as great but you see them in a big game, when the pressure is really on, and they're not there. Not Roro. The bigger the match the better he played.**

In contrast Brock James has acquired a reputation for inconsistency in big matches. That's a little unfair. He's had some poor games but he's also had some good ones when the pressure is on. As a fly-half he's got great vision, has a very good long pass to get outside the centres, and his tactical kicking has got us out of troubles on numerous occasions. He's let himself down defensively at times, that's the one area where he lacks a bit of steel. It was hard to know with Brock how the setbacks affected him. He's a pretty reserved guy, who doesn't give much away in terms of emotion.

Thibaut Privat is another man who keeps his emotions to himself but he's the man I'd want to take into battle before any other. No question that Thibaut is the best second-row I've played with, followed by Nathan Hines. The thing about Thibaut is that he does all the hard things right and doesn't make a lot of noise. When you're locking the scrum it's essential that you have confidence in the guy alongside you. If you're camped on your try-line with minutes to go and the opposition have a five-metre scrum you need to know that the guy next to you in the engine room is going to give it his all. Not one backward step. I always had that belief in Thibaut. I'm just glad I never had to play against him because it's one of the most chilling sights in rugby, to see Thibaut coming at you, 50 centimetres off the ground, like a flying coffin. I've seen him chop many a man in half.

I've been fortunate to play with some brilliant hookers, and Mario Ledesma and Benjamin Kayser are the best. Mario probably just edged it as a thrower. He could always put the ball in the right spot and he had a great shape on his throws. He was also very good at dropping it right on you as you went up. I've jumped in the middle and at the front of the line-out and I don't really have a preference. Line-out jumping was never the strongest facet of my game but I worked hard to improve it over the years, and with experience jumping becomes easier. You learn how to get

quickly in the air and when to make the right calls. There is a different technique to jumping at the front and the middle of a line-out. The further you go back the less time you have because you have opponents around you trying to get in the air as fast as you. So it's about reading the body positions of the defences and getting free of your opponents as you're about to jump. Whereas front-jumping is a lot more about having a good connection with your hooker so you get the timing of the jump just right.

Thibaut and Damien Chouley are my closest buddies in rugby. They're both fine men and great players. Damien lived just down the lane from us in Clermont so we hang out together a lot and one summer he came on vacation to Canada and I took him round all my haunts. I've felt for Damien in recent years because the demands placed on him by France and Clermont have been immense. In the 2015-16 season, for example, he played 12 Tests for France and 17 matches for Clermont - every one a big game. It's too much.

Other teammates at Clermont who stand out are Pierre Mignoni, who left us for Toulon in 2009 before going into coaching. It's no surprise Pierre is doing well in his new role. As a player he broke the mould of French scrum-halves. He was really focused, trained hard and paid attention to every facet of his game, from nutrition to passing to every technical aspect. You would always see Pierre doing a little extra training at the end of a day, not something you can say about a lot of French players.

When Pierre left his successor was Morgan Parra, our little general. It's fair to say Morgan isn't one of life's natural trainers but I tell you what, he's a tough little bastard! When he arrived from Bourgoin I took one look at him and thought 'he's too small'. He looks like he'd break in two if he tried to tackle a forward. But Morgan's a great competitor and his aggression around the ruck makes him almost like a third flanker. His contribution to Clermont has been huge, as was that of Julien Bonnaire. Off the field Julien is a really funny guy, a very dry and cynical sense of humour. He's not your typical big loud brash guy but he carries himself with great style and dignity. On the field he's one of the best back row forwards that France have ever produced.

The one guy I had a little trouble figuring out was Napolioni Nalaga. He arrived at Clermont a year after me and soon became a cult figure. During his eight seasons at the club he scored tries for pleasure with opponents unable to handle his size and speed. Check out the stats - 104 tries in 154 European and Top 14 matches. It's a staggering number.

As a man Nalaga was a bit of an enigma. He can play the dumb Fijian when it suits him, but in fact he's very switched on and understands everything that's going on. There was a lot of hot air from Clermont when he left the club for Lyon in 2015. Initially Nalaga was linked with a lucrative move to Toulon and that caused the ASM president, Eric de Cromières, to go public with his 'disappointment'. Yet in the same interview in La Montagne, Cromières questioned my future at Clermont. "The club has a strong attachment to this player who's never let us down, who's always given his all," he said. "But at the end of the day can we reasonably re-sign a player beyond 37 years old?"

So let me get this straight, Eric: you moaned about Nalaga's possible departure to a club offering him more money, yet in the next breath you thank me for a decade of service but regret I'm probably too old to merit a contract extension. Seems Eric expected total loyalty from his players right up until the day their services are no longer required. To be honest Clermont were lucky to hold on to Nalaga for as long as they did. From 2008 onwards he was probably the best wing in France but he wasn't getting what he was worth. Toulon and then Lyon came along, threw decent figures at him and the money turned his head. What's wrong with that? There comes a point when every player has to realise that this life lasts only for a certain length of time. You need to make a good living and when someone offers you big money, hell, you're going to think about. I know for sure that Clermont pays less than a lot of other clubs. They think that because they have a great infrastructure, a loyal public and play good rugby that they can afford to pay players a little less. Maybe in some cases but the rise of Toulon, Montpellier and Racing in recent years has undermined that approach. It was disappointing, too, to hear some Clermont fans boo Nalaga when news of Toulon's interest became known. I expected better from the Yellow Army. Rugby is a professional sport and a player's shelf-life is getting shorter and shorter. Why shouldn't he move to a club where his talent will be properly rewarded? People don't think less of people in the business world changing jobs because they've received the offer of more money and bigger bonuses.

*

The two seasons from August 2008 to June 2010 were probably Clermont's peak years under Vern Cotter. In the summer of 2007 he'd brought on board Joe Schmidt, a fellow New Zealander and now coach of Ireland. Joe is awesome. He was exactly what the squad needed when he arrived in 2007. Vern was transforming the pack but the one area that needed improvement was the backline and Joe soon went to work. He brought a level of precision to the whole squad that made huge impact and between them they formed a formidable partnership.

Joe was a schoolteacher in an earlier life and it tells in the way he's able to impart technical knowledge in a simple and easy-to-understand way. He's never afraid to criticise but does so always in a constructive way and, like Vern, he has high standards that he expects to be met. The other good thing about Joe and Vern is that they never talk down to you, which isn't always the case with coaches.

When Vern had been appointed head coach at the start of the 2006 season he introduced a five year programme. He told us that if we all bought into it, made the necessary sacrifices and put in the required work, then it would start to bear fruit. It turned out he was right, but before we could experience the pleasure there was still some more pain to endure.

We finished third in the Top 14 regular season of 2008-09, nine points behind Perpignan and Toulouse, who were the most consistent performers throughout the championship. That meant a semi-final against Toulouse in Bordeaux and an opportunity to avenge our defeat in last season's final. We did, winning 19-9, a victory that was inspired by Brock James. He scored 13 points, including five for one of the best solo tries you're ever likely to see. Collecting a pass just a couple of metres inside the Toulouse half, Brock thread a path through their defence, accelerated and chipped the ball past Maxime Medard, beating the full-back to the touchdown. It was Brock at his best, matched in the second-half by me at my worst. My tackle on Yannick Jauzion was so late it would have been fined five bucks if it had been a library book. It wasn't a dangerous hit, just a stupid one, and if you watch the tape of the tackle you see me looking straight away at the touch judge. I knew I was in trouble and it was one of those yellow cards that not even I could argue with. Fortunately my rush of blood to the head didn't have serious consequences and we won 19-9.

So once more we were on our way to Paris. It was final number ten and our opponents were Perpignan, who had beaten Stade Francais in their semi-final. The Catalan club have a history every bit as rich as Clermont's, and they too had failed to give their passionate supporters the success they deserved. Twice in the previous decade (1998 and 2004) they had reached the Top 14 final only to lose, and their last success was way back in 1955. Though they had a talented backline, including a young Maxime Mermoz and the reliable South African Gavin Hume at fly-half, it was the Perpignan pack that was their strength. Their cosmopolitan front row of the great **Nicolas Mas, one of the best tight-heads in the business, the Romanian hooker Marius Tincu, and England loose-head Perry Freshwater was a mean trio, while in the back-row they had a couple of real bruisers in**

Jean-Pierre Pérez and Grégory Le Corvec. Sandwiched between them at No8 was a young, fresh-faced Damien Chouly, who looked as if butter wouldn't melt in his mouth.

The match unfolded in a horribly familiar way to the 2007 final against Stade Francais. We dominated the first-half, turning round with a 10-6 advantage, and then limply subsiding in the second-half. A Brock James penalty were the only points we scored after the break as Perpignan coasted to a 22-13 victory thanks to a try from David Marty and 11 points from the boot of Jerome Porical. Distressing would be an understatement.

Our third consecutive defeat in the final and our tenth overall. What the hell was wrong with Clermont? It's a question that everyone connected with the club has asked themselves in recent years. For what they are worth, here are my thoughts. There were times when I felt some of the squad weren't giving it their all. I want to think that every one gave the best of themselves in the big matches, and went to the maximum of their limits, but the fact we have lost four Top 14 finals and two Champions Cup finals in the last ten years suggests that perhaps they weren't.

Why not? Some of the squad, particularly the French boys, are just too comfortable. Playing for Clermont is a good life. The club has wonderful facilities, the fans are always behind them, win or lose, and maybe sub-consciously, this creates a comfort zone. You want for nothing at Clermont so why push that extra yard?

Clermont is a very self-contained town. It's in the middle of nowhere, quite isolated, dominated by the Michelin company and the rugby club. So the players are revered wherever they go in the town. They're Gods. This creates a comfort zone that isn't there in a club like Racing 92 or Saracens, where the players, once they leave training are hardly recognised. I think complacency has crept into Clermont over years, as it has Toulouse, and while the squad is so talented that they can get through most games successfully when it comes to the crunch matches they lack the edge of other big teams. That missing one percent can make all the difference in a final. It might manifest itself in a variety of ways: a missed tackle, a pass that doesn't go to hand, a bad decision in the closing minutes.

The reason why Toulon had that glorious period where they won three consecutive European titles and the 2014 Top 14 crown was because they recruited players who were very talented but also interested only in winning - and above all prepared to push themselves to the limit and beyond in the process: Jonny Wilkinson, Carl Hayman, Bakkies Botha, Ali Williams, Chris Masoe, all players ready to die for the cause. They've all now retired and look what's happened to Toulon.

But this complacency comes from the top at Clermont. I'll be blunt: during my eleven years at the club I wasn't sure the directors and administrators were that bothered by winning trophies. They were more concerned with the brand and the balance sheets. What's important to a lot of the suits at Clermont is having a pretty club where things tick along nicely each season. We always reach the play-offs, do well in Europe and the fans keep coming through the turnstiles.

In my time at Clermont the club didn't change in the way it needed to. Of course they'll rubbish these words when they read them, and mock me for suggesting they don't want to win trophies but the statistics speak for themselves. My criticism isn't directed at Franck Azema or his coaching staff, they're striving to win, but they're not being supported in the boardroom. Clermont didn't recruit the players they could have recruited because they wouldn't make the effort to sign the very best. The fundamental problem at Clermont is that the board of directors are nearly all Michelin men with the exception of Jean-Pierre Romeu, who's also the only one who has played rugby at the top level, even though it was in the 1970s.

So what I'm saying is that there is no one in the Clermont boardroom who is from a dynamic company, who has had to fight his way to get to somewhere. They're all from the same mould, and have a very measured and direct way of doing things. That's the Michelin mould and it may work in the French business world but it hasn't in the rugby world. No one brings new ideas or inspiration into the boardroom, and more importantly in terms of a sports organisation there is a lack of hunger and fire. The directors of the club are content to stay in their comfort zone, enjoy the prestige that comes with their position, and continue to be big men in a small town.

The supporters deserve better.

*

We opened the 2009-10 championship with a 38-27 win away at Bourgoin. There were a couple of tries for Napolioni Nalaga and Brock James kicked 17 points. Brock had been the top points-scorer in the Top 14 since the 2006-07 season but he now had a serious contender for that mantle: Jonny Wilkinson. The great English fly-half, dogged by injuries for a number of years at Newcastle, had signed for Toulon that summer. His first appearance for Mourad Boudjellal's boys was a dream with Jonny landing 17 points in the win over Stade Francais.

The Toulon president has his critics, some pretty loud ones, but I like the way he shakes things up. You can only admire the guy for the way he transformed Toulon with his money and ambition. He' attracted enemies because he dared take on the status quo - and the old boys who run French rugby are as conservative as they come - and they didn't like having their noses put out of joint. It's a bit like the guys who run Clermont. Too many administrators in French rugby, whether it's the FFR, the LNR or the clubs, believe it's a job for life and they're entitled to do as little work as possible.

Mourad's been called crazy but a little bit of crazy can be good. Same applied to Max Guazzini when he became president of Stade Francais in the 1990s. Cheerleaders? Pink flowery shirts? Nude calendars? He was laughed at initially but he revolutionised rugby. He brought a showbiz touch at a time when it was still very much a grey, conservative sport run by guys from the amateur era.

Guys like Guazzini and Boudjellal had made their fortunes by taking risks, and it shouldn't have been a surprise when the Toulon president decided to gamble on signing Wilkinson. In his first season Jonny guided his new club to the final of the European Challenge Cup, playing some of his best rugby in years and more importantly staying injury free. That was until the final of the Challenge Cup against the Cardiff Blues when he injured his back early in the second-half. Toulon were in command at 13-6 when Jonny hobbled off but without their playmaker they collapsed to a 28-21 defeat.

The week before that European final we had met Toulon in the semi-final of the Top 14. They'd seen off Castres without too much trouble in the quarter-final while we had just edged out Racing 21-17. It wasn't a pretty match. We played with a lot of tension and Brock James endured a torrid first half with his kicking. Morgan Parra took over the duties and that proved decisive as he landed five from five. When his confidence is up there are few better scrum-halves in the world than the little general.

So it was Toulon in the semi-final at **Saint-Etienne, which is also a real cauldron to play in,** and a match that turned out to be one of the greatest in the history of the Top 14.

It was a slow-burner. Jonny got Toulon on the board after three minutes with a penalty and then Anthony Floch levelled for us a few minutes later with a drop goal. The two sides exchanged penalties, Jonny landed a goal, and then I should have got the first try on the stroke of half-time. We were camped on the Toulon line in the right-hand corner and I picked up the ball and drove for the line. Sonny Bill Williams stopped me and sort of rolled me over. As he did I lost my bearings. If I'd planted the ball down, as I could have in the couple of seconds before Toulon hands came in to hold it up, it would have been a try but I thought I was still behind their try line so I tried to recycle it.

Trailing 9-6 at the break we were still confident, and in the second period we began to assert our dominance up front. We put the squeeze on Toulon in the set-piece, won three penalties and Morgan Parra landed them all. Then on 68 minutes **Davit Zirakashvili barged his way over for the game's try. For the first time we had had pulled ahead of Toulon but they showed a glimpse of the steel that would come to characterise the club in the coming years but staging a fantastic late rally. First Sonny Bill scored a try and then with two minutes left on the clock Jonny struck a fifty metre penalty to level the scores at 22-all**

It was every player's worst nightmare: extra-time. In a match of that physicality both teams were drained at the end of normal time so the prospect of twenty additional minutes was daunting. It was the first and only time I've played 100 minutes of rugby, and I hope never have to again. At my grand old age now, I think that's unlikely.

We struck first, Brock landing a penalty on 90 minutes to put us 25-22 up. Then, and making a mockery of all those who said he didn't have the big-game temperament, Brock dropped a goal to put us 28-22 ahead. A minute or so later I arrived at a breakdown, saw Julien Malzieu free on his left wing and flicked up the ball into his hands. I'd like to say it was a brilliant piece of vision on my part but it wasn't. I was just executing what we'd been taught by Vern and Joe, which was to play whenever we could, keep the ball moving and when we had the chance to counter-attack, do it.

Julien was a substitute so he was fresher than most, and he showed Toulon a clean pair of heels as he kicked ahead and raced down the touchline to score what the

Yellow Army believed was the match-winning try. It was a great moment for Julien, who had established himself in the squad the same season I arrived at Clermont. For the next five seasons he developed into one of the league's best wings, playing regularly for France, and scoring a bucketful of tries. Unfortunately ever since 2010 he's been plagued by injuries and he's never been the same player. That was his moment, however, and so we thought it was ours, but Toulon somehow lifted themselves. They were like one of those movie villains: no matter how many times you batter them they just keep rising from the dead.

Trailing 35-22 with six minutes to go they worked their way into our 22 and Fabien Cibray, on for Pierre Mignoni at scrum-half, wriggled over for a try that Wilkinson converted. We now led 35-29 and Toulon ripped into us, attacking us in waves, with Jonny directing operations with his usual unflappable precision. This was the man who seven years earlier had won the World Cup for England with a drop goal in the last minute of extra-time so who knew what he had up his sleeve this time. With a minute remaining they moved the ball from left to right, just inside the Clermont half. I summoned up the last of my energy to tackle Sonny Bill but he managed to offload the ball and it went out to Gabiriele Lovobalavu on the right wing. He evaded one tackle and suddenly the pitch opened up before him. I remember staggering to my feet, exhausted, and looking down the field as Lovobalavu sprinted for the corner. He was going to score and then it would be down to Wilkinson to land the touchline conversion. But just as he began to lunge for the line Gonzalo Canale pulled off one of the great covering tackles. The siren sounded and we were in the final.

*

The key moment in the 2009 Top 14 final didn't occur on the pitch. It didn't even occur on the day of the match. It happened the night before at the referee's briefing. The squad was informed that there would be zero tolerance for foul play in the final. This was the showpiece day in the French rugby calendar and the referee told us he would not hesitate to show a red card to any player who stepped out of line. Fair enough.

The first fifteen minutes of the final were mayhem. Two minutes into the game and Julien Bonnaire was showing a bite mark to the referee on his forearm; then Mario Ledesma gets laid out and a few minutes later it's my turn. I was packing down on the flank in the final with Thibaut Privat and Julien Bonnaire in the second row, and as we stood up from a collapsed scrum, I got struck flush in the face from my old friend Grégory Le Corvec. It was his hardest punch, or at least I think it was, and I took it with barely a murmur. They had a laugh about it later on Canal Plus, expressing their admiration that I didn't flinch. What the TV analysts didn't find so funny, and nor did I, was the failure of the officials to punish Perpignan.

Normally I would have knocked Le Corvec's head off for that unprovoked punch. But I had the ref's words still ringing around my head. Any violent play will result in an automatic red. So I took the shot and thought, 'you're going off, Greg'. It had to be a red card. It happened in clear view of the touch judge. Not a thing. It was typical French refereeing. They talk big and then bottle the brave decisions because they lack the balls when they're out in the middle.

There's no doubt in my mind that we **weren't on the knife edge for that 2009 final. We were a little bit behind it and that was because in the back of our minds we had the ref's stern warning from the previous evening. No one wants to get sent off in a final in front of 80,000 people, right?**

But far from being a tightly controlled final, it was a case of anything goes. The winner was the side that wanted it more and was prepared to go to any lengths to win, and in 2009 it was Perpignan.

The fact the 2010 final was a repetition of the previous season's worked in our advantage. We weren't going to be caught cold again by any team, and certainly not Perpignan.

Curiously, however, there was no referee's briefing before the 2010 final, which made the 2009 talk all the more strange.

We arrived in Paris a couple of days before the final and checked into our hotel, which was just outside the city. On the Friday a few of us went shooting with the

GIGN cops [Le Groupe d'intervention de la Gendarmerie nationale], a trip organised by Elvis Vermuelen, who knows someone in the service. That was awesome, and it was a privilege to get a brief glimpse of the professionalism and expertise of the GIGN. We went to their shooting range in the forest and blew off about 1,000 rounds. It was great fun, and the perfect way to pass the day before the final. When we were on the range we were so focused on what we were doing that we emptied our heads of rugby anxiety for a few hours.

Even though it was our fourth consecutive final we didn't have any set routine for the Friday evening. The boys whiled away the hours as they wanted. Some played pool, some cards, others watched TV and a few of us had a game of petanque in the hotel grounds. For some players, like Morgan Parra and Alexandre Lapandry, it would be their first start in a Top 14 final, and the nerves were immense. For five of us it was our fourth consecutive start and the emotion was more of determination to get our hands on the Bouclier de Brennus. Aurelien Rougerie, Thibaut Privat, Mario Ledesma, Brock James and myself had all been named in the starting XV and so there was an onus on us to call on all that experience the next day.

It's been a huge honour to play in four Top 14 finals but I do have one complaint: the kick-off times. I'm not a fan of evening matches. For me the ideal time to play is the traditional mid-afternoon. I like to wake up, have a late breakfast and then get my game head on. But with the 21h kick-offs you have to hang around until about six o'clock before you get in the bus and head to the ground. It's a long day when the hours drag so slowly.

When the match started we took control straight away, and this time, thankfully, unlike the other years we didn't relinquish our authority. Morgan Parra got the first points of the match with a penalty after ten minutes and then a few minutes later we scored what turned out to be the only try of the game.

Lapandry won quick line-out ball on our ten-metre line and the ball was moved along the backline into the hands of Rougerie. He made the initial break, offloaded to Anthony Floch on the halfway line and he surged up to the Perpignan 22 where he found Brock James in support. He sidestepped his way to within a few metres of the tryline before he was hauled down. I came charging up, try-line tantalisingly close, and took a pass from Parra on the short side. I put my head down , and came in on an angle, but the Perpignan flanker, Jean-Pierre Perez, took me low by the knees. We recycled the ball and this time Morgan went right, running a perfect line before flicking the ball back inside for Nalaga to score the try with me half a metre behind to give him a final shove over the line. Ironically, Nalaga hadn't scored his usual glut of tries that season for Clermont - the one in the final was just his eighth, compared to 21 the season before - but never was there a more important one.

Just a quick word about Alex Lapandry, whose take in the line-out started the movement that led to the try. I am amazed that Alex hasn't won more caps for France. When he made his Test debut in 2009, aged 20, I expected him to be there for years. But he went on to win just a handful of caps and last played for Les Bleus in 2014. I can't understand why. I don't think there's a flanker with a bigger engine in France. He's everywhere. He's a text-book tackler, good in the line-out, great hands, reads the game well and just keeps going and going. He regularly makes 20 plus tackles in a game, sometimes nearer thirty, and if I were coach of France he would be my first-choice flanker.

Nalaga's try, and Morgan's conversion, put us 10-0 up, and after we'd kicked another penalty we had to weather a fightback from Perpignan. Two penalties in quick succession from Jerome Porical reduced our lead to 13-6, but he then missed two relatively easy kicks at goal either side of half-time. Those misses convinced me more than ever that this was our year. In the 2009 Porical had been our chief tormentor, keeping Perpignan in the game with his goalkicking and territorial kicking, but he looked out of sorts in 2010.

We took a 13-6 lead into the break, which was the same margin we'd enjoyed 12 months earlier, and things could have got off to a disastrous start in the second-half straight from the restart. Perpignan kicked off and there was a misunderstanding between Privat and Ledesma. They left the ball for each other, it bounced, and could so easily have fallen into the grateful hands of the onrushing Perpignan pack. But Morgan came to the rescue. He may not be the biggest but he's one of the bravest and he leapt to claim the bouncing ball, receiving half the Perpignan pack on top of him for his troubles. But we cleared our lines and from then on we resumed control. Thibaut was replaced by Julien Pierre on fifty minutes, a tactic we'd been employing for a season or two. It worked well because Julien has a hell of a motor and his arrival always added some extra impetus in the final quarter.

Morgan kicked another penalty on the hour mark, extending our lead to 16-6, and then with twelve minutes remaining Floch dropped a superb goal. Some Clermont fans pinpoint those three points as the moment they knew the title was ours. For me that moment was earlier in the second half when we had a maul and drove Perpignan about twenty metres upfield. All they could to stop the drive was bring it down illegally. There was a bit of pushing from them, some swearing, and at that moment we sensed that we'd just sapped the last of their strength from their bodies and mind. We told each other: keep playing, we've got them, no let up like previous years.

I don't remember much of the last few minutes. I learned later that Thibaut and Mario Ledesma retired to the changing room for the last ten minutes because they couldn't bear the tension. Out in the middle I was vaguely aware of the emotion being generated by the tens of thousands of Clermont fans. It's hard to explain. I was so concentrated on what I was doing that I didn't glance at the clock or into the crowd. But I could start to feel a shift in atmosphere, perhaps a slight lightening as the Clermont fans began to shed 74 years of misery.

The funny thing is I have absolutely no recollection of the final whistle. I couldn't tell you where I was on the field or who I grabbed. The first memory I have is walking towards the tunnel and seeing in slow motion pandemonium erupt. Some boys were on their knees crying, others running around screaming, it was an amazing experience.

Once we'd collected the shield we went back down to the pitch to show it off to the supporters - the long suffering Clermont supporters. They were good moments. The Yellow Army are the soul of Clermont. I may not think too highly of the club's directors but the fans are the best in the world. The sacrifices they make to follow the club. The Auvergne isn't the richest region in France and the last decade in particular has seen some tough economic times, but the fans keep coming. That's what had hurt most about the previous defeats, seeing the despair on the faces of the supporters, and feeling we'd let them down.

There's one supporter in particular I admire, the man they call 'Le General'. He's a little guy with grey hair and a moustache. On the video of the 2010 final, as the cameras film our celebrations, you see me go over to the General and we embrace and share a few words. He's a beauty of a guy. I don't think the General has missed a game for forty years, and he above all other fans was responsible for me understanding the devotion of the supporters. I went to a restaurant in Clermont to meet some friends and by coincidence the General was having his retirement party in same venue. We had a drink together and that's when he told me that at the start of each season he takes a little loan from the bank and then maps out his schedule for the season. He plans everything down to the minutest detail - hotels, petrol, meals, even the cost of the road tolls - so it can fit into his season's budget. When you hear first-hand of that level of passion and commitment, it makes you even more motivated because you're not just playing for yourself and your teammates, you're playing for tens of thousands of supporters who live, eat and breathe Clermont.

That night we went as a squad with families and friends to a nightclub in Paris. I had a couple of friends over from Canada, ex teammates from the Capilanos, which added to the fun, and I just felt a little sorry for Jennifer because there we were drinking champagne through the night but she was pregnant with Maelle.

There was no sleep for the players, we carried on through to breakfast and then it was straight on the team bus to the train station. There we had our own train waiting for us, which was very cool. There was a disco car, a restaurant car, a movie car, a lounge car and a bar car. The families head to the lounge car to sleep and the players made themselves comfortable in the bar car, and we stayed there drinking until we reached Clermont. It was quite a fete. No player let himself down by sloping off to the lounge bar for a sleep. We all stayed until the bitter end, royally entertained by Martin Scelzo, our Argentina prop. He's a force of nature on and off the field. Quite early on in the journey south he'd acquired a conductor's hat, and he kept popping up in strange places over the course of the next three hours. Behind the bar, on the bar, under the bar. There was a camera crew on the train and needless to say Martin took the camera from them and started interviewing the players in his unique South American style.

As we approached Clermont no one was quite sure where we should get off. At each station we passed as we got nearer to home, fans were on the platform waving as we went by and the excitement just seemed to build. In Clermont itself about 15,000 had descended on the station to welcome us and I think the authorities were worried about controlling the crowd.

So they decided to stop the train outside of town and let us out, but even there were about 1,000 people waiting. We fought our way onto the bus and headed towards the stadium but by this time word had spread that we descended the train and were on our way to the Marcel-Michelin. I'll never forget those scenes as we edged through the thousands of people outside the ground. It was a huge party. Some were crying, others laughing, it was indescribable. Once in the stadium we swapped the bus for an open-top bus, but when we tried to leave we couldn't, there were just too many people. So the cops had to encircle the bus with a length of rope and walk us out of the stadium, down the road and into town. That meant a five minute journey took about one and a half hours. Not that we minded, we just carried on partying. I remember when we got to the Place de Jaude looking down and seeing one old guy, he must have been in his 70s, with tears pouring down his face. He was just utterly overcome with emotion.

Once the open-top bus tour finished, the boys headed to the local TV studios for one of the more amusing live interviews. Not me. I was done by then. Let's just say I went home to 'freshen up' for a few hours before the next round of celebrations began.

A nice touch from Clermont in the months that followed our victory was their loaning out of the shield. Players could reserve it for a weekend or an evening and I did that on one occasion, taking it to show off at the Stadium Bar, which was my local when I first moved to Clermont and lived in one of the club's apartments. I knew the owner well, and a lot of the regulars, so we set up the shield in the corner, took a few photographs and sank a few beers.

Chapter thirteen

After the triumph of 2010 I came down to earth with a bump, and a ban, the following season. And not just one ban. In October I was given a crazy seventy-day suspension for stamping against Saracens. A few days after serving my time I returned to action with Clermont and in my first game back I did something stupid and was hit with a forty day suspension. I copped some stick for that. All my various misdemeanours over the years were brought up in the media, and I believe I became quite infamous on youtube. I've never watched myself on youtube, by the way. I'm not proud of any my yellow or red cards - though then again most of them weren't deserved.

But I was aware that I was being described as a 'thug, 'an enforcer', a 'nutter'; all the usual cliches.

Listen, I've never set out to illegally hurt anyone on a rugby field. I play within the spirit of the sport, and when I've run in to trouble it's because I've either retaliated or I've just gone ever so slightly over the edge of the line that separates legitimate aggression from excessive physicality.

I've never gouged, bitten or butted, and nor have I purposely stamped on an opponent. Similarly, I've never run up to someone, like Pascal Pape did to Jamie Heaslip in a Six Nations match a few years ago, and dropped my knee into their back. Gutless stuff like that, you never do, and anyone who does, then it takes you down three or four pegs in my eyes. It's why I've got no time for Pape, average in every sense of the word. In contrast, someone like Bakkies Both; he played the game in a similar hard-nosed style to me.

I played my formative rugby as an amateur in Canada, New Zealand and Wales, and it could be pretty wild west rugby at times. You get stuck under a ruck or maul in New Zealand and people shoe the shit out of you, and so they should. You shouldn't be there. I carried that philosophy with me when I became a professional. If an opponent was lying on the wrong side, trying to slow up our ball, I gave him some boot. I didn't stamp on his head, I rucked him out of the way. If I see someone enter a maul illegally I'm going to fly in there and smoke them with my shoulder. I go in hard but legally. But, sure there have been a few times when I've got my timing wrong, or misjudged the hit, and ended up with a yellow card.

There's no doubt rugby has become more and sanitized because it's such a big ticket item nowadays Top 14 matches are transmitted round the world and the powers-that-be want a clean, fast game. Of course, the best way to speed up the game is to bring back rucking - rucking New Zealand-style as I experienced in 2000. But that's never going to happen. Too dangerous and too unpalatable so instead we have to endure the confused mess that is the breakdown.

The season I had in Wales - where they also liked their rucking - I hardly ever got into trouble. The Welsh play hard but generally fair. So it was a shock when I moved to France. First, I have to say that the game in France is a lot cleaner now than it was when I arrived in 2003. It was vicious back then. Every week there would be cases in the Top 16 (as it was then) of biting, gouging, stamping. And mass brawls involving 20 or 30 players were a regular occurrence. The violence has diminished over the years, and we saw the fuss that erupted in September 2016 after a brawl between Grenoble and Brive that resulted in three red cards. That was a throwback to a previous generation yet to judge by the hysterical media coverage you would have thought French rugby had never before seen anything like it.

It's good that the game's cleaner. I'm now a parent and I wouldn't want my kids playing a sport where players bite each other or stick their fingers in each other's eyes. The FFR and the LNR are to be congratulated on clamping down on violence. I'm not sure their motives were wholly altruistic. Their new-found intolerance of foul play may have had more to do with the money that began flooding into the sport from broadcasters and sponsors: blue-chip companies aren't going to invest millions if they think their name could be tarnished with appalling scenes of violence every weekend.

Another explanation behind the decline in violence is the evolution of the sport. Rugby is so much faster in 2017, so much more structured and organised, than it was at the turn of the century that players haven't got time to stand around gouging and punching. If you're trading blows with an opponent instead of taking up your position in the defensive line then that could be the hole through which the opposition come.

And finally, the ubiquity of the television camera means there is really no hiding place for players out in the field. A good example is Brive fly-half Mathieu Ugalde, who last season was banned for fourteen weeks for gouging Armand Batlle as the Grenoble player dived over for a try. His defence was that his fist was closed; yet the TV freeze frame, widely circulated on social media, showed an extended finger in Batlle's eye. Ugalde might have got away with his gouge in another era but as I said, in 2017 it's virtually impossible for any wilful act of foul play to go undetected. Ugalde deserved his punishment but there are times when the camera angle can actually make something appear worse than it is. A hand accidentally comes into contact with someone's face, for example, as two players contest a line-out, and if that one frame is frozen, and uploaded onto twitter, it can create a false impression. I've never understood gouging. It's brutal, the lowest of the low, and only a coward would put his   fingers into another player's eyes with the intention of hurting him, perhaps blinding him for life. It's sick shit.

I speak from experience. The first time I was gouged was my debut season in France, playing for Grenoble against Agen. I'd only been on the field a few minutes as a sub, and we were mauling, trying to get over the line. I recall that the maul went to ground. I went down trying to clear the guy out and the Agen prop, this old guy, a really dirty bastard, got hold of me and rammed his fingers into my left eye. He burrowed in two, so deep the fingers actually split the eyeball. I might not have been able to see anything in my left eye but in the right one I saw nothing but red mist. I went nuts. Turning round, I bent this old bastard backwards over the ruck and just started filling him in. And I filled him in good. By the time I'd finished he was covered in blood. The ref sent no one off. He saw my eye, he knew what had happened, so he let me exact revenge, and then he told me to calm down.

In Monday morning's video session Jacques Delmas, the Grenoble coach, accused us of playing like girls. He pointed to me, my eye still red and swollen, and said:
'Thank God we had the Canadian Sheriff to sort things out'. The boys thought that

was hilarious so thereafter I was known at Grenoble as the Sheriff. I can laugh about it now, but the first time you are gouged properly is a scary moment. You really do think you're eye will be damaged for good.

The other time I remember being badly gouged was during the 2007 Top 14 final against Stade Francais. No surprise when I tell you it was Remy Martin. Whenever you played that guy you feared being trapped at the bottom of a ruck. And if you were you just scrunched up your eyes and prayed you didn't feel Martin's fingers trying to prise them open.

Please don't think I was ever intimidated by Martin. I wasn't. I just like my eyes as they are. I've never been intimidated on the rugby field. Sure, I've been scared of screwing up in a play, doing something that lets my buddies down, but in terms of being physically intimidated by another human being, no. I like playing the guys with the baddest reputations. I see it as a great challenge and it fires me up to be more aggressive myself.

Nor am I much of a talker on the field. Verbal abuse, banter, whatever you want to call it, it isn't a tactic of mine. I'm more a reactionary sort of guy, going at it in heat of moment.

In my first season at Grenoble I got only one red and one yellow. All things considered, I was quite well-behaved. I let myself down in the second season. The eight yellows I copped were clearly way too many. It remains my most ill-disciplined season. In fact the second highest number of yellows I received in one season were the three I got (along with a red) playing in my first year at Clermont.

Was there a link between the eight yellows and the off-field chaos at Grenoble in 2004-05? No, that would be a weak excuse on my part. What was going on at Grenoble was frustrating but I can't blame it on my poor discipline. It was more the fact that I was too fired-up when I played. I was aware, being my second season, of the level of violence in the French championship, so I went out to meet fire with fire. There was also an element of wanting to prove myself. I was trying too hard and that sometimes spilled over into excessive aggression.

When I have been sent to the sin-bin I've used the time to refocus. I watch the match and tell myself

when I get back on I have to make up for the ten minutes I've cost my side. I'm usually left alone. I don't need a coach to come and tell me off. On only one occasion can I recall anything being said to me, and that was a message from Vern Cotter passed to me in the dug-out during the 2009 Top 14 semi-final against Toulouse in Bordeaux. It had nothing to do with my crime but was a tactical message for when I went back on.

The first time my reputation crossed the Channel was in December 2007 in a Heineken Cup match against Wasps in High Wycombe. The English club were the reigning European champions and they had a hell of a side: captained by the great No8 Lawrence Dallaglio, they had another member of the 2003 World Cup-winning XV in full-back Josh Lewsey, and several internationals including Raphael Ibanez, Paul Sackey and Tim Payne, a prop who'd won a few caps for England.

An hour into the game Payne and I clashed. We both arrived at the breakdown close to the touchline. He lashed out at me, then grabbed me and wrestled me to the ground. I flipped him over and gave him a bit of a going over. Meanwhile it was kicking off as players piled in. Martin Scelzo got involved in a scuffle with James Haskell, and as they settled their differences a member of the crowd leaned over and tried to hit Martin with a rolled up match programme. He actually hit Haskell. It turned out that the programme pummeller was 62 year old Alan Black, an RFU Official, former captain of Wasps and the then leisure manager at the club. Poor old Blackie. The media had a field day, and he was given a dressing down by the RFU and banned from attending Wasps matches for the rest of the season. It was just an instinctive reaction from an ex-player. But remind me when I'm old never to stand to close to the action - just in case I have a rolled-up programme in my hand.

I was subsequently banned for four weeks by the Heineken Cup organisers, which went some way to appeasing the many folks who believed I deserved red for punching Payne. I obviously disagree. I have never walked off the pitch, having been shown a yellow card, thinking 'Phew I'm lucky it wasn't red'. The school of hard knocks...I went to the school of hard done by! I always believe I've been treated harshly. That's probably why I never watch clips of myself on youtube. For me I'm innocent until proven guilty but unfortunately for the refs I'm guilty until proved innocent. Which brings me to Paul O'Connell.

Chapter 14

"It's bubbling over. O'Connell is right in the middle. Cudmore is unloading and it's all kicking off...Cudmore and O'Connell...it's getting pretty ugly now. Cudmore can be feisty and proving it again there."

So ran the live commentary on Sky Sports, describing the moment that me and Paul O'Connell came to blows in December 2008. It was a Heineken Cup pool match between Munster and Clermont and it's the fight for which I'm best remembered. There's a case for saying it brought down the curtain on the old school punch-up, certainly in European rugby. Nowadays if players ever clash, it's just pushing and shoving. But me and Paulie traded some good blows that day in Limerick. I've said it before but I'll say it again, Paul O'Connell is one of life's good guys. He's a gentleman to his fingertips and no one encapsulated the passion and ferocity of Irish rugby the way he did for so many years. But why the hell wasn't he sent off, too! When Chris White, the ref on the day, spoke to his touch judge about the fight he said of O'Connell: "He's involved but he hasn't done a punch the same way." Eh! What sort of gibberish is that?

But I'm getting ahead of myself.

Clermont went into the match desperate for victory. We'd had a shocker in our opening Pool 1 match, losing 32-15 to Sale Sharks, before recovering to win our next two games, away at Montauban and at home to Munster. The victory against the

Irishmen at the Stade Marcel-Michelin meant that whoever won the return fixture at Thomond Park would likely top the group.

We knew we were in for a day to remember. The Munster fans - the 'Red Army' - are probably the most vocal supporters going and they've proved the inspiration for Clermont's own 'Yellow Army'. On this day there were 25,000 spectators and nearly all were screaming themselves hoarse for the Munstermen. I love Irish crowds. The banter is awesome and you often hear some great one-liners. I've always relished playing at grounds like Thomond, because it gives you all the motivation a player needs: the best way to shut up the crowd is by getting stuck into their boys.

I hadn't any previous with Munster or O'Connell, although there was a little antagonism between the two sides because of events the previous season. Clermont and Munster had been drawn in the same Heineken Cup pool in 2007-08, and the Irish had handed out a serious thrashing at Thomond Park, running in five tries in a 36-13 win. We'd actually started the match the stronger of the two sides, but the game was transformed in the eighth minute when the referee, Nigel Owens, showed Vilimoni Delasau a yellow card for not rolling away at a ruck. It was a tough call, and as one or two Clermont players queried the decision, Ronan O'Gara took a quick penalty and sent a cross kick into the corner that resulted in a try for Shaun Payne.

I missed that match through injury, as I did the return fixture at Clermont when we won 26-19 despite having three men sin-binned. Four yellow cards in two games, and it's fair to say there was a feeling of injustice within the Clermont squad. You could say the same about most French clubs. When it comes to 'Anglo-Saxon' referees - by that they mean anyone who speaks English, regardless of whether they're Welsh, Irish or South African - the French have an innate sense of perfidy. Most of the perceived injustices are a figment of their imagination but there have been a few times when French clubs seem to get penalised for offences that British or Irish clubs don't. It doesn't help that the majority of Home Nations referees don't speak a word of French. You would have hoped, being professional refs, they'd take it upon themselves to learn the language. They don't need to be word perfect, just enough to communicate. It's a question of respect above all else. Imagine if a French ref rocked up at Thomond Park to officiate Munster against Northampton and spoke to the players in French. They'd be uproar.

So while this was my first match at Thomond Park I'd been told what to expect from the boys. It was going to be a full-on 80 minutes. Unfortunately my involvement lasted only 18 of those minutes.

The opening minutes were uneventful. No niggle and no points. Clermont had a line-out a couple of metres inside our own half. **Benoit Cabello threw to me in the middle and I won the ball but it wasn't clean. It bounced a metre to the side of our scrum-half, Pierre Mignoni, and he knocked it the ball on as he tried to gather it. Referee Chris White blew his whistle and in the same instant Pierre got thrown to the ground by the Munster prop, Marcus Horgan. That caused a reaction among the Clermont forwards, who came to Pierre's rescue, and the Munster pack then got involved. I found myself in a bit of a rough and tumble with O'Connell, our hands round each other's throats. I could hear the ref manically blowing his whistle, and then Paul and I glanced at the touch judge. He had his flag out in front of him so I knew something was up, and I remember thinking 'If I'm going out I'm taking this guy with me, so I let fly with a few. Paul cracked me back a couple of good ones and it ended as an old-fashioned punch-up.**

As I said, I don't go looking on the internet for the stupid shit I've done but that particular fight has been hard to avoid over the years. People love showing it to me. It's quite funny, seeing me and Paul rolling around on the grass with Chris White squealing 'let go, let go of him'. Eventually we were separated and led back to our respective corners by our teammates, while White consulted with his touch-judge. I was expecting the same punishment for me and O'Connell. In Canadian hockey, if two guys get in a fight, then they're both sent off for the same amount of time. It's logical.

So I wasn't too happy when I got a red and he got a yellow. How did that work? Some people have said that I got red because I threw the first punch but that's a lame excuse. We were both willing actors in a bit of fisticuffs, we both threw some

shots and we both should have received the same punishment. And for White to say of O'Connell that **"he** hasn't done a punch the same way", that just makes him sound ridiculous. A punch is a punch.

Intriguingly, I found out later that the touch judge in that Munster game was Roy Maybank. Five years earlier he had refereed the Canada v USA match in Vancouver, the game where I scored a try at the death that would have won us the match, but he disallowed it because he had been poorly positioned. I'd torn off my headgear in frustration but I hadn't been aggressive towards Maybank, either in the heat of the moment of afterwards. The moment the final whistle sounds, that's it for me. Game over and don't carry any grudges into the dressing room. But did that incident influence Maybank in 2008? You'd have to ask him but if you watch him on the video, talking with White, he's sure sounds pretty keen for me to receive a red card. It's too bad if he was carrying a chip on his shoulder five years later.

As the television pictures show I wasn't too happy when I saw the different colour of cards. I can't honestly remember what I said to Paul as we walked off but it's safe to say I wasn't inviting him to tea and cakes. It was a little more abrasive than that, probably something along the lines 'let's go again'. I got some grief from the Munster fans as I walked off. But who can blame them? I'd just bloodied their golden boy and they let me know they weren't happy. Some of the language was quite strong but it had no effect. Sticks and stones, etc,

Ever since that afternoon a lot of people have assumed Paul and I have this simmering hatred for one another. Nothing could be further from the truth. By the end of the match the anger had subsided and that evening we had a good chat over a beer. We've met each other many times since, on and off the field, and it's always good to catch up. I'm just sorry that Paul's Test career ended with his going off injured against France in the 2015 World Cup. Not only did that rob Ireland of their talisman in the quarter-final against Argentina but the hamstring injury proved so serious that it forced Paul into premature retirement. He had been due to play for Toulon for a couple of seasons and I was relishing the prospect of one final clash with Paul in the Top 14. After all, this time around, he would be in the red of Toulon and I in the yellow of Clermont. Finally, justice!

But whatever the rights and wrongs of my dismissal, the fact was I'd left my teammates a man down with an hour to play. The Munster fans bayed for blood, and initially it looked they'd see the humiliation they craved. A try from David Wallace helped Munster into an 11-3 at half-time but Clermont staged a superb fightback in the second-half with a penalty from Brock James and then a converted try from Julien Malzieu putting us 13-11 up going into the final quarter. A miracle seemed possible but Munster drew on all their experience in the last five minutes, scoring two quick tries to snatch a 23-13 victory.

The way the boys had reacted to my red card was magnificent and I felt pretty uncomfortable after the game because I'd let the team down. I apologised to them but there were no hard feelings on their part. They understood how these things happen.

I had to wait six years for my revenge but they say it's a dish best served cold. In the 2014-15 competition we were drawn once more with Munster and this time at Thomond Park we came away with a 16-9 victory. We were the first French side to win in Limerick and I had one of my best matches in a Clermont shirt. We took the lead in under a minute, our pack driving over Fritz Lee from a line-out, and thereafter we strangled the life out of our hosts. I put in some big hits on O'Connell - all perfectly legal, I hasten to add - and that win, coupled with our victory at the Stade Marcel-Michelin a week later, ensured Munster failed to qualify for the quarter-finals of the Champions Cup for only the second time this century.

Chapter Fifteen

I was banned for five weeks for the Paul O'Connell fight. He wasn't even cited. Work that one out.

It wasn't the first time, and it wouldn't be the last, that I had cause to curse a Heineken Cup **disciplinary hearing. I've encountered a few clowns in my rugby career and most have worn suits and sat on disciplinary panels. I draw a distinction between French panels and European rugby ones. You get a fair hearing in France, or a fairer one, at least. When I've gone to Paris to state my case in front of the LNR they have one or two ex-players on the panel, people who still have a feel for the sport and its pressures. These guys really go into bat for you if they see that you've done something stupid rather than a act of deliberate and violent foul play. As I've already said, I've never bitten ears or gouged eyes and if I have been in trouble I've told it straight and they appreciate that. The French disciplinary panels also** understand they if a player gets himself on the wrong side of ruck then he's going to get some shoe.

A case in point was the red card I received in a Top 14 match against Perpignan in September 2009. That was a fiery match containing some residual bitterness from their victory over us in the final a few months earlier. I came on as a substitute and was pretty fired-up, and I caught Jerome Porical a little late as he cleared to touch. It wasn't a dangerous tackle, just slightly late, and as I got to my feet I was accosted by Jean-Pierre Perez. I hit him with a right, and fair play to him, that thick head of his took it pretty well. His knees sagged but he didn't go down. Suddenly out of the corner of my eye I saw Robins Tchale-Watchou charging across the pitch. I could see he had only one thing on his mind, so I threw the first punch and he then launched a couple my way. I got a red and Tchale-Watchou was given a yellow. I pulled a face and made a couple of disbelieving noises but trudged off without further ado

I always think I've been hard done by but I always accept the referee's decision. It's not always easy - that Munster game in particular - but you've got to respect the decision. Rugby is built on respect and the moment that foundation cracks the sport is in trouble. It concerns me to see the amount of talking-back that now goes on out in the middle. Players now are definitely questioning referees and chirping away at touch judges more now than they did ten years ago. It needs to stop. Refs should have zero tolerance for any talking back. Penalise any player who gets in their face. It comes down to education from an early age. From mini rugby to school rugby to club rugby, you must be drilled to respect the referees. They're actors in the games just like the players. None of us are perfect, we all make mistakes, but we have to accept those mistakes, hard as it may be. One of the more startling incidents in recent years involving a referee concerned one of my old Clermont teammates, Viktor Kolelishvili. He shoved Wayne Barnes during a Champions Cup match against the Ospreys in 2016.

I understood why Viktor did it, because Barnes was standing in the channel down which the Ospreys would probably launch their attack, and teams always look to try and use the referee as a blocker. But you never lay hands on the referee. I was out injured at the time, watching the match on the TV, and I couldn't believe what I'd seen. Barnes handled the situation pretty well, I think he was in a state of shock, and Viktor got some serious piss taken out of him from the squad the following week. He didn't take it very well. Most of the Georgian boys are really good guys but when you take the piss too much, they don't really like it.

But back to Perpignan. I was sent off and though I left the field muttering to one and all, on reflection it was the right call to show me the red card. The ref had also spotted my punch on Perez. Robins and I got fair hearings in Paris. He took a 10-day suspension and I got twice as long.

A year later I was back in front of a European Professional Club Rugby (EPCR) disciplinary panel to answer charges of stamping on Jacques Burger during a pool match against Saracens. In my opinion it was a crazy call to even cite me. I wasn't punished at the time and I didn't think anything of the incident. Burger had fallen under feet of the Clermont pack in a maul. He got some boots because he shouldn't have been where he was. But no one, me included, deliberately stamped on him. It was old-fashioned rugby and Burger couldn't take it. He required five stitches in his mouth after the game but we exchanged a few words, I said I hoped he was OK, and that was that. Next thing I know I'm cited - and only me - for stamping.

The hearing was in Dublin on October 13 and it was just me and the Judicial Officer, some Welsh guy called Simon Thomas. He's a lawyer, and he's quite a reputation, by all accounts, but he sure as hell wasn't a rugby player. It's a joke that lawyers oversee rugby disciplinary panels. Most of them are clueless with no understanding of the pressures on the players. They just apply the letter of the law but without taking into account the nuances of the game. The whole system needs to be shaken up so that the people who sit in judgement on disciplinary panels have an empathy and an understanding for the game.

It's time World Rugby brought an ex-player onto all disciplinary panels so that players get a fairer hearing. That might also end some of the grotesque inconsistencies we see all too frequently. And a lot of these inconsistencies, it has to be said, seem to adversely affect the Tier Two nations. The one that sticks in my mind was the five week ban handed to Samoa wing Alesana Tuilagi during the 2015 World Cup. The guy did nothing wrong. He just ran hard and fast like all Samoan boys do, and the Japanese player, **Harumichi Tatekawa, got his head on the wrong side when he tackled. That's his fault, not** Tuilagi's. Yet in the same week Australian flanker Michael Hooper received just one week for a shoulder charge on England full-back Mike Brown. What was the more dangerous and cynical act? Just about everyone in the rugby world bar the disciplinary officer thought Hooper's. Fiji also treated harshly at the 2015 World Cup, losing three players to bans, but England's Tom Wood and Sam Burgess both escaped censure for reckless acts. **Simon Thomas certainly gave me the impression that he had no clue about the difference between hard play and deliberate foul play. The following is a transcript of what I said in the hearing:**

"I rejoined a retreating maul in a defensive position where Saracens were advancing. In my efforts to halt this movement I was trying to gain some kind of positive foothold to stop the momentum. The maul then broke up and I fell to the ground with one or two of the Saracens players. It was clear by their reaction that they felt something had occurred but also by my reaction that I was surprised by this. I do not contest that there was contact between my foot and the side of Mr Burger's face, but I do strongly contest any accusation that this was a deliberate stamp. I feel that this is borne out in the video clips that were forwarded to the club and I spoke to Mr Burger after the game to reiterate this and see if he was OK. (I additionally sent him a letter on Sunday wishing him well)."

In the slow motion video clips Burger was seen falling backwards as the maul advanced. As he went down, he tried to take me down with me, grabbing the collar of my jersey. I had hold of Burger's right shoulder and was at such an angle that I brought my left leg down in an attempt to shoe him out of the way. Burger was just lying there, preventing us from trying to stop the Saracens' maul.

I was found guilty of deliberately stamping, "on the balance of probabilities", and my testimony was described as "unreliable". It was only unreliable because I admitted I had made contact with Burger with my boot but I was trying to shoe him

and not stamp on him. A former rugby player would have understood the difference. Thomas didn't. He came out on top in a one to one because he's a trained lawyer. I tried to put my case but he was too skilful for me. It wasn't really a fair fight but then what do disciplinary committee's know about equity?

What disappointed me most about that day was having to sit there and listen to two fellow professionals trying to get me banned. Nobody can say Jacques Burger didn't put his body on the line for Nambia and for Saracens during a great career but boy, for a tough guy, he could sure whine. We had a beer after the game, shook hands, and then he sets out to assassinate me. Same for his little buddy, Deon Carstons. I don't Carstons can spell ethos, let alone apply it. The letter that the Saracens prop sent to the disciplinary committee exaggerated the whole issue. I couldn't believe what I was hearing when the letter was read out.

"I was holding onto Jacques Burger in a drive. Jacques fell to the floor. He was lying on his back. Clermont lock Jamie Cudmore lifted his left leg and brought it down aggressively onto Jacques' face. I was positioned above Jacques and in my opinion Jamie Cudmore lifted his left leg higher than is normal and brought his foot down directly onto Jacques' face."

Burger and Carstons behaved like a couple of little schoolboys telling tales in the school yard. Pathetic.

I was banned for nine weeks. A decision that was absolutely ridiculous. Simon Thomas had the decency to acknowledge that there was element of "provocation" in Burger holding onto me as he fell to the ground, and he also stated in his conclusion that had "he found that this had been a deliberate stamp to the face or head [the ban] would have been significantly higher". So in other words I was banned for nine weeks for shoeing Burger out of the way. The crowning indignity was an additional one week ban because of 'previous suspensions'. Angry? That's an understatement. There have been several instances in my career when I was approached, either by Canada or Clermont, and asked to give evidence against a fellow professional in the hope of seeing him banned. I've always refused. It's not in my nature to go around telling tales and trying to get people into trouble. If you've got differences to settle, you settle them out in the middle, you don't sneak around behind people's backs in the following days and weeks. And you certainly don't write whiny little letters to the headmaster.

In fact the only evidence I've submitted to a disciplinary panel was in March 2010, when I wrote to the LNR in defence of my bosom buddy Gregory Le Corvec. He and I had clashed again, and he'd been charged with gouging. But he hadn't. You know when you've been gouged, you can feel the fingers working their way into the eyeball, but in this case Greg's hand had inadvertently scrapped across my face. When he heard he had been charged with gouging he gave an interview in which he declared: "I swear on the head of my children, on the heads of all those my dear to me in the world, that at no one moment have I touched his eyes". That's one of the things I love about Greg, he's a pass master at melodramatics!

Then he said that he hoped I would "tell the truth" and that the LNR would call me and ask if I'd been gouged. So I wrote a letter to them and explained that I hadn't been gouged by Greg. Not that it did much good as Greg still got slapped with a 40-day ban. He called to thank me and I replied it had been a pleasure to try and clear his name.

Obviously I was ready to help him out off the field but on it Greg and I were still smashing each other. Like I've said, I like Greg, got a lot of respect for the guy, but at the same time I did enjoy whacking him.

But there's a time and a place for hitting Greg and it probably wasn't my first match back for Clermont after completing my ten-week ban for shoeing Jacques Burger. But I couldn't help myself. Just after half-time I arrived at the breakdown, went to clear out some Perpignan players and there he was, Le Corvec. Boom! I hit flush him on the jaw with a hammer of a right hand. He was all over the place, and that was last the game saw of Greg. Unfortunately it was the last match I played for a while. This time I had little to offer by way of defence when I was called in front of an LNR disciplinary panel.

I copped a forty-day ban. Added to the Burger ban it meant that I would sit out a third of the 2010-2011 season. There were suggestions in some media that I was becoming a "liability" to Clermont and perhaps it was time I was moved on. That was never a serious possibility but nonetheless I realised I had to address my indiscipline. Whether or not I was always at fault my absences were letting down the club, and in particular, my teammates. And I was also letting down myself.

I went to see a sports psychologist. I was a little sceptical at first, unsure it would work. I still had vague recollections of those sessions at the Maples Adolescent Treatment Program in Burnaby, and they hadn't done me much good. But I was a kid back then, and now I was man with a wife and child so I was prepared to give it a go.

Seeing the psychologist was one of the best moves of my rugby career. We discussed why I reacted the way I did. I explained that I didn't bubble with frustration and then explode. It was always pretty sudden. If you look at most of my transgressions over the years they've been instantaneous. It's how I am. Every human reacts differently to situations but essentially it's Fight or Flight, right? I'm the former. And I wasn't just fighting, I was getting the first blow in. It was the same story growing up in Squamish; if I felt threatened I had to go from zero to 100 faster than the other guy. I had to take control.

The psychologist listened and I was expecting the usual crap about fighting is wrong, etc, etc. But he said, 'I don't have a problem with you hitting someone on the rugby field. If you want to punch someone, go ahead and punch them. But not before you've imposed yourself in other areas. Because if you're punching opponents before you've imposed yourself in the set-piece or at the breakdown then you are not doing your job'.

That statement caught me by surprise. The psychologist was the first guy who told me it was OK to punch an opponent. But. And the 'but' was when it clicked for me. I saw exactly where he was coming from. Before I could fight I first had to make ten good tackles and I had to carry ten times. Then my reward would be to fight. But of course I became so preoccupied with those tasks, of imposing myself on the game legitimately, that I lost the urge to fight. In purely animalistic terms I was marking out my territory in a way that was just as aggressive but within the rules of the sport. That was my rugby epiphany and I have never received another red card.

Of course, I didn't just change overnight. I knew now how I had to channel my aggression but there were still opponents looking to provoke me. Everyone knew my reputation and saw my temperament as the chink in my armour. The psychologist told me if ever I found myself in a flashpoint situation I had to drop to one knee and re-do a bootlace. That helped. So, too, did writing the names of Jennifer and Maelle on my wrist strapping. Becoming a father plays a part in mellowing most men. It's not the best image for a child to see their dad knocking the shit out of someone. All these little tricks worked and my last suspension was a 20-day ban for a little contretemps with Stade Francais scrum-half Jérome Fillol in 2011.

If my on-field behaviour has created a few lurid newspaper headlines I've never stepped out of line off the pitch as a professional. My conduct off the field is something that's very important to me. I'm a professional athlete and I have a duty to act as one. Sure, I like a beer now and again, but only at the appropriate moments and I've always gone out of my way to avoid trouble, and that includes local hard men looking to make a name for themselves.

The only time I've come close to a fight in public was one afternoon in Clermont a few years ago. My mum was over on vacation and Jennifer and I took her shopping. The girls had bought a bottle of wine for supper and they were walking ahead of me a few metres, chattering away as they crossed the road. A car slowed to let them cross and then suddenly revved its engine. The punks in the front had wanted to scare my wife and my mum, and they achieved their aim. I was mad as hell. As the car drove on I told the occupants what I thought of them. The car braked and out jumped the guy in the front passenger seat. He came towards me, one of his hands behind his back. Weapon of some sort, I thought. No problem. I advanced thinking that I'll have to drop him before he has a chance to use the weapon. I could hear my mum - my poor mum, no doubt having flashbacks to a decade earlier - yelling 'No, Jamie, don't fight, please'. That made me glance at the girls and what I saw made me laugh out loud. Jennifer was moving round behind this guy clutching the bottle of wine as if to clock him. Atta girl! The sight of this laughing Canadian guy coming towards him spooked this punk. He turned and ran, dropping his 'weapon' as he fled, which turned out to be nothing more than a spit stick.

Chapter Sixteen

I was delighted when I saw the draw for the 2012-13 Heineken Cup. Exeter, Llanelli Scarlets and Leinster. I knew little about Exeter, who were then a relatively unknown force in England, but I was looking forward to renewing acquaintances with my old friends in Wales. As for Leinster, well, Clermont had a score to settle with them.

They had assumed Munster's mantle of the most powerful side in Ireland, and for a time they were Europe's most dominant club. They'd won the Heineken Cup in 2009, 2011 and 2012, an unprecedented spell of success at the time.

We'd met Leinster in the semi-final of the 2012 tournament, what was a superb game of rugby at the Stade Chaban-Delmas in Bordeaux. It Clermont's first appearance in a Heineken Cup semi-final, and the match contained only one try it was a tense and thrilling contest with a cruel climax for Clermont. Trailing 19-15 with two minutes remaining we drove at the Leinster line, the pack edging closer with each charge. The ball was then moved right, to Wesley Fofana, who rode the tackle of Gordon D'arcy to reach out and touch the ball down for the try. The place erupted. Wes leapt to his feet and was mobbed by us all. Seconds later the ecstasy turned to agony. Referee Wayne Barnes had gone upstairs to the video ref to check the try was good. It wasn't. Wes, who had his back to the try-line as he hit the ground, thought he had touched down, but the ball had actually hit his upper arm and then bounced forward without making contact with the turf. It was the correct call by the video ref, and it broke all of Clermont's hearts.

We wanted revenge the following season, and we got it, beating Leinster home and away to knock them out of the competition at the group stage. The 15-12 win at the Stade Marcel-Michelin was particularly satisfying as it was Leinster's first defeat in the Heineken Cup in 17 games. A week later was the sequel, in front of nearly 50,000 fans at the Aviva Stadium in Dublin, and a brilliant display of goalkicking from Morgan Parra saw us home 28-21. The Little General scored 23 points with the only try coming from Fofana, a sweet moment for him after what had happened the previous season.

We topped the pool and played Montpellier in the quarter-final, destroying them 36-14 in a five-try rout. That set up a semi-final with Munster. Paul O'Connell and his boys were no longer the force of a few years earlier but they were still a very dangerous prospect. It was Munster's 10th appearance in a Heineken Cup semi-final and our second. Yet we were very confident.

Vern Cotter had us peaking at just the right moment so that a European and domestic double was a real possibility. Clermont and Toulon were out in front of the rest in the Top 14 and we had our sights on two finals.

Munster stalwarts such as Anthony Foley, Denis Leamy and Alan Quinlan had retired but their successors, the likes of Tommy O'Donnell, Peter O'Mahony and James Coughlan were good players, if not quite in the same bracket as their predecessors.

The Clermont side had also changed quite a bit since our first meeting with Munster in 2008. Martin Scelzo, Mario Ledesma and Thibaut Privat had moved on, Elvis Vermeulen was coming to the end of his career, and their places had been taken by Damien Chouly, Ben Kayser, Julien Bardy and Nathan Hines.

Our pack was too strong for Munster in the semi-final, that's what won us the game. We also had the boot of Morgan Parra to punish their indiscipline, and his three penalties complemented the converted try of Napolioni Nalaga after nine minutes. It was hearts-in-the-mouth time moments before Naps crossed the try-line because he ignored a four-man overlap. If he'd butchered the opportunity he would have been run out of France but Nalaga has a hell of a nose for the try-line and he cut back inside and powered in under the posts.

I only lasted the first-half, succumbing to a hand injury, but the boys resisted a ferocious Munster fightback that included a try from Denis Hurley. We had reached our first Heineken Cup final, and it would be an all-French affair against Toulon at the Aviva Stadium in Dublin.

Toulon had got to the final the hard way, overcoming Leicester 20-15 in the quarter-final and then beating Saracens in the semi-final. Jonny Wilkinson had scored all their points in that 24-12 victory but he wasn't the only danger man in the Toulon side. The huge South African veteran Bakkies Botha was playing some of the best rugby of his outstanding career, as was Australian centre Matt Giteau, and their back-row of Chris Masoe, Juan Fernandez Lobbe and Danie Rossouw was world-class.

But for all Toulon's talent, we dominated them for the first hour. There are some matches where you sense from the start you have the edge physically on your opponents and this was one of those occasions. We controlled the game, all aspects of it, from the set-piece to the offensive plays. One of our best moves of the first half was started by Sitiveni Sivivatu, who danced through the Toulon defence and found me in support. I drove forward another few metres and then Morgan Parra moved the ball right to Lee Byrne, who accelerated into the Toulon 22.

We continued to test the Toulon defence for the rest of the half and Brock James came within a hair's breadth of scoring five minutes before the break when he kicked ahead and beat Chris Masoe to the touchdown. The only question was: had the ball gone across the dead-ball line before Brock got downward pressure? The ball was actually on the line when Brock touched it down but the whitewash is out so it was no try.

Our inability to turn our dominance into points in the first-half was a concern but

Vern Cotter told us during the break to keep playing and the points would come. The number of tackles being made by Toulon would surely wear them down. Sure enough within ten minutes of the restart we had scored two tries and raced into a 15-6 lead. Both tries were beauties. Most of the backs had a hand in the first one, Sivivatu and Fofana - both of whom had great games - stretched the Toulon defence down the right-hand touchline, before the ball was moved across field into the hands of Nalaga. Naps still had a lot of work to do when he took the pass from Aurelien Rougerie but he made it look so easy. For such a big man, Naps has incredible finesse and it's that blend of grace and raw power that makes him such a special player.

Five minutes later a wayward kick from Sebastien Tillous-Borde bounced into the hands of Nathan Hines. He offloaded to me, I made a couple of metres, and then Parra fired a pass to Brock James. Brock received the ball on the halfway line, saw that the Toulon defence was rushing up in a line and so sent up a perfectly weighted chip kick over their heads. Rougerie raced ahead, collected the ball, and despite the attentions of a couple of Toulon tacklers, got the pass away to Brock. He still had twenty metres to run but Brock had enough gas to get over the try-line and score a richly-deserved try. He's come in for some criticism over the years but few people can read a game of rugby like Brock. Parra converted and it looked like game over. That's the moment when we should have closed down the match but we kept on playing, and in doing so we allowed Toulon the opportunity to claw their way back into the game. Wilkinson kicked a penalty on the hour mark to reduce our lead to 15-9 and then three minutes later came the decisive moment. I hold my hand up and admit I was partly responsible. Fofana made the initial break and was brought down a couple of metres before the halfway line. I arrived to clean out the Toulon defenders but I cleaned them out too well, allowing Lobbe the chance to step over me and snatch the ball out of Sivivatu's grasp as he went to pick it up. What Lobbe did next was brilliant. He spun round and saw that the two teammates nearest were both forwards, so he looked for another option and he spotted Delon Armitage in acres of space on the left wing. Once the ball was in Armitage's hands it was a race to the line between him and Brock James. There was only ever going to be one winner and there was always ever going to be one outcome to the conversion Even though it was wide out, Wilkinson drilled it between the posts to put Toulon 16-15 ahead with fifteen minutes to play. We shouldn't have tried to run from our 22. We should have kicked the ball deep down field, and then moved up in a good defensive line and closed out the game.

When Toulon scored their try a lot of weight went out of a lot of guys. I could feel it. We'd been in so many finals, and lost nearly all of them, that when we went behind in a match we had dominated up to that point, some players began to waver and lose belief. It's a familiar story with Clermont over the years but in general it's a French trait. When something goes wrong on the field, too often teammates turn on each other, start bickering and throwing up their hands in frustration. When was the last time you saw New Zealanders arguing among themselves? In the Anglo-Saxon world there's a greater team ethic; things sometimes go wrong in a match, that's rugby, but in Canada, Wales and New Zealand, the three countries I've played in, you don't shout at each other, you support each other. It's got better over the years in France but the esprit de corps isn't as good as it could be.

It was a shame that some of the gloss was taken off Toulon's win by the furore that erupted over Delon Armitage's gesture to Brock as he ran in the try. Personally, I couldn't see what all the fuss was about. I was running after Delon so I got a good view of him sticking out his tongue and waving. I had no problem with that. Hell, I'd do the same thing probably, if only I could run as fast.

There was a lot of bullshit written in the papers about Delon being 'disrespectful' and betraying the spirit of the game, but people need to understand the pressure players are under these days. This was the European cup final, and Delon - who I don't know other than having played against him a few times - was on his way to the try-line. He was happy he'd got one over on us and let him celebrate the way he wants. Players should always respect the rules of rugby but the rules don't say you have to play the game poker-faced and never celebrate a try. And people are very selective when they criticise players. Delon took a lot of heat for that try, yet a few weeks later George North did something similar playing for the British and Irish Lions against Australia, and hardly anyone batted an eyelid. Yet Delon was still getting booed by supporters, and not just Clermont ones, two seasons later for his gesture. I was disappointed at Clermont fans for the way they treated Armitage. He didn't deserve that. He scored the winning try and Toulon won the game. That's sport. Accept it and move on.

Much has been made in recent years of the rivalry between Clermont and Toulon. Most of it is whipped up by the media, and carried on by the supporters. I always found the players to be a good set of boys and we had some pretty tough battles that created a healthy respect between the squads. It was pretty hard to be sociable after that Heineken Cup defeat, though. We knew we'd thrown it away, let slip a game that we had dominated for an hour. I recall going upstairs to the post-match function in the Aviva Stadium, sharing a few words with the Toulon players, and then just wanting to get the hell out. We left the function first and headed downstairs to the coach. Toulon left a few minutes later and unfortunately our coach was behind theirs' so we had to sit and watch as they emerged with the trophy. There was no gloating on their part, in fact they kept their celebrations muted out of respect for us. Nonetheless to catch sight of the trophy was demoralising.

We had no time to wallow in self-pity. A week after the Heineken Cup defeat we faced Castres in the semi-final of the Top 14. Clermont had finished top of the regular season table, seventeen points clear of Castres, who were fourth, and we were the overwhelming favourites to reach the final. Though they'd beaten us 16-13 at their ground, we had thrashed Castres 37-10 at the Michel-Michelin. The semi-final was in Nantes and I wasn't involved. I'd hurt my hand in the Heineken Cup final and an x-ray revealed a small fracture. Even if I had been fit I doubt I would have made much of a difference to the outcome. Castres won 25-9. We were blown off the park, our morale still in pieces following the lose to Toulon. It was a wretched way to end a season that just a week earlier had promised so much.

Chapter Seventeen

The 2013 Heineken Cup triumph was the first of three consecutive titles for Toulon,

the first time a club had achieved the feat. Mourad Boudjellal, the millionaire publisher of comic books, had taken a 51 per cent stake in the club in 2006 and gradually transformed Toulon into the strongest team in Europe. It had taken time, and there had been setbacks, but the appointment of Bernard Laporte as director of rugby in 2011 was a key piece of the jigsaw. 'Bernie' had the strength of character and coaching pedigree to win the respect of the star-studded squad, and, of course, to attract fresh stars to the Cote d'Azur. When Toulon won their third European title in 2015 - and once again Clermont were the fall guys - they had the likes of Bryan Habana, Ali Williams, Drew Mitchell, Juan Smith and Leigh Halfpenny - in their XV, along with Bakkies Botha, Carl Hayman and Juan Fernandez Lobbe, who had all played in the 2013 final.

Yet there's no doubt in my mind who the most important recruit was to Toulon - Jonny Wilkinson. There have been more naturally talented fly-halves in the world than the quietly-spoken Englishman, yet none with such an extraordinary work ethic. By dint of practise and attention to detail, Wilkinson became of the greatest names in the history of the sport, and when he arrived in Toulon the French had never quite seen anything like it.

Jonny - or 'Sir Jonny' , as the French press still call him - remains a God in Toulon and a hugely respected figure in France. Why? Yes, he's a good guy, but mainly because the French realise they'll never produce a player like him, certainly not a fly-half, who's prepared to sweat blood in the pursuit of perfection. France have had some superb fly-halves in the last decade - Frederic Michalak, Camille Lopez, Francois Trinh-Duc, David Skrela, Jules Plisson - but none have been able to find the consistency to establish themselves as an international fly-half. Michalak, pound for pound, is probably a more gifted player than Jonny, but compare their Test match stats. Fred scored 436 points in 77 matches for France, and Jonny 1179 in 91 appearances for England.

It's a sad reflection on France that Michalak is their record points scorer. Four hundred and thirty six points, that's not many, not when set alongside the other major powers. Dan Carter - who since arriving at Racing 92 has assumed Jonny's mantle of the idol of the Top 14 - scored 1598 points; Neil Jenkins of Wales, Ireland's Ronan O'Gara and Diego Dominguez of Italy all passed the one thousand mark, while the Scots, South Africans and Australians have kickers who have 800 points or more.

My point is that goalkicking requires practise, patience and perseverance, and those three traits are sadly deficient in the majority of French players. Technically, the French national squad has been in decline for a number of years. Even the basics, like catching an up and under, or passing the ball down the backline, appears beyond the capability of many French players. How is this possible? France is the nation that gave the rugby world the word 'flair', and yet in the 21st Century Les Bleus have become, certainly under Philippe Saint-Andre, a laughing stock. That a country with their resources should finish in the bottom half of the Six Nations in five consecutive seasons - 2012 to 2016 - is a joke.

The brutal truth is that professionalism has exposed the amateurism of too many French players. And not just the players: the coaches, administrators, the whole damned structure.

But let's start with the players. I'll never forget when I first arrived at France to play for Grenoble, the boys all drank coca-cola after a match to 'boost' their recovery. I couldn't believe it. They were adamant it was the best thing to drink immediately after the match. I told them it was about the worst thing they could drink, it was all sugar. There was still in those days very much a culture of the post-match piss-up, what the French call the *troisieme mi-temps*. Even in my first season at Clermont I remember a few occasions staggering back to my apartment at about four on the Sunday morning after a hell of a night out on the town. That culture has gradually been phased out in recent years. Above all, we **just don't have time for it now. Games are so physically and mentally draining, and recovery time so limited, that almost as soon as one game is over you have to start preparing for the next. It's a shame in a sense, that the social side has diminished, but the sport's professional, we're very well paid, so it's important we behave professionally.**

Having said that, the French approach to fitness training is also something to behold. When I'm with the Canada squad the conditioning coach will tell us: 'OK, today we're going to do X number of sprints and then Y number of tackles', and so we do the work without a word and when it's done it's done. You very rarely hear any player whining 'how much do we have left to do?' or 'how much longer to go?'. Same goes for my experiences playing club rugby in New Zealand and Wales.

But in France it's a completely different mindset. The boys arrive for training and pinned to the board are details about the morning's fitness session. Straight away you'll hear 'Aw, hell, do we have to do that?' There's a distinct lack of enthusiasm from the start. The French guys will stand around for twenty minutes, a few will ask if it's really necessary, and they only start training with the greatest reluctance. They'll do the fitness but never without having first moaned. Obviously there are exceptions to the rule, and you're never going to hear guys like Alex Lapandry and Damien Chouly whine, but in general French players are among the more unenthusiastic when it comes to training. It's the same among young players as the guys who are in their late twenties or early thirties. The France Under 20 squad continually under-perform in the World Championship each June. Don't get me wrong, they have some very talented guys, but too many of them are physically under developed compared to the English or South Africans because they don't do enough work in the gym. And then how many of the Under 20s go on to establish themselves at their clubs? Not many. And don't give me the old excuse about too many foreigners in the Top 14. Sure, there are a lot, probably too many, but the fact is coaches are obliged to look overseas because the quality of young homegrown players simply isn't good enough. Too many France U20 players think that they've made it when they reach that level. On the contrary that's when the work really starts. Again, there are exceptions and one of the young guys at Clermont who really impressed me was Judicaël Cancoriet, the flanker who made his debut in 2015-16 aged 19. He puts in the effort and gets his reward.

Canada isn't a major rugby power but we are a very good sporting nation and we use every facet of sports science to give us a leg-up and make us competitive with countries who, in terms of player resources, dwarf us. In contrast France is still steeped in tradition. I have a friend back in Canada, Joe McCullum, who's a very good conditioning coach, and he told me not so long ago: 'Tradition is the most dangerous thing in sport because it makes you complacent'. What does that mean? That people will say 'but this is the way we've always done it so we'll keep doing it'. If you do that you eventually will hit a wall and go no further. The France national team have hit that wall. When Guy Noves replaced Saint-Andre as coach after the disastrous 2015 World Cup a huge amount of expectation was heaped on his shoulders, but in many ways Noves epitomises the malaise within French rugby. Look at how Toulouse declined in the last five years of his reign. He got overtaken by time. Maybe I'm speaking too soon. Perhaps Noves will reverse the decline of the France team. We'll see over the next two or three years. One other observation about the France squad in recent years - stop chopping and changing.

There's an incredible statistic for the number of half-back combinations that Saint-Andre used during his four years in charge - 17 different combinations in 45 Test matches. Madness. How the hell is any side going to find a rhythm and stability if the half backs are changed practically every other game? Similarly, the French are alone among the major rugby powers in having this strange belief that half-backs are interchangeable. I could not believe it, during the 2011 World Cup, when Marc Lievremont suddenly started playing Morgan Parra at fly-half. Frederic Michalak and Jean-Marc Doussain have also switched between fly-half and scrum-half in recent seasons. It's madness. These are pivotal positions that require completely different skills and decision-making, yet in France people think 9 and 10 is more or less the same thing. For me, and for most Anglo-Saxons, the fly-half is the one who calls the shots. Look at Jonny Wilkinson, Dan Carter, Ronan O'Gara, Jonathan Sexton, Stephen Jones, etc. They dictated how their side played. In France it's the scrum-half who runs the show. Name me the last France fly-half with real authority, who was able to exerted control. Probably Gérald Merceron, who I played against in 2002 shortly before he retired.

The same inconsistency in selection applies in the France back-row where Saint-Andre and Noves have switched players with bewildering regularity. In contrast, look at the All Blacks. They rarely chop and change, and since becoming coach of England at the end of 2015, Eddie Jones has brought a consistency to the selection that resulted in the 2016 Grand Slam - their first for 13 years.

In short, France is certainly playing catch-up with the rest of the world. Rugby has been professional since 1995 but it's only in the last three or four years that everyone is starting to train properly in France. I'm talking about little details, like activating their bodies to get ready for training rather than just going straight into it, and having a pump session on the Friday to get a testosterone boost for Saturday's match. I saw a big improvement in my last years at Clermont with more thought being put into the whole training process, and a greater emphasis being placed on recovery sessions, which are so important nowadays with the physicality of the game.

The problem in France is that rugby is a huge **old boys' network that is very conservative. I touched on it earlier but there are these layers of hierarchy in French rugby that stifle development. But I'm afraid that's the problem with France in general, whether it's in rugby or at Michelin or in most companies. It's all very hierarchical and nobody steps out of their zone. Everyone has their job title and that's all they do. No one is encouraged to do any extra work or come up with fresh ideas. That's totally alien to me, as a North American. We're always trying to excel and progress, and make ourselves the best we can. The Anglo-Saxon model is not perfect, but the French model sure isn't perfect, but too many people in France, particularly from the older generation, sneer at the rest of the world and believe the best way is the French way. Well, I've got news for you, it's not.**

I've always pushed myself to the limits, going back to my adolescence. Whether it was soccer, skiing, snowmobiling or lifting weights, I wanted to push the limits of pain and suffering and see what I was truly capable of.

We get one crack at life so why not push ourselves to the maximum 24/7? In a rugby context the harder you work in training, particularly individual training, the better you'll perform on game day. I'm sponsored by the American sportswear company UnderArmour, and they also take care of Michael Phelps, the greatest Olympian of

all-time. Prior to the 2016 Olympics they produced a TV commercial with Phelps, which gave a tantalising glimpse of the training regime that made him the swimming champion he was. The words that appeared on the screen at the end were: 'It's what you do in the dark, that puts you in the light'. So true. It's easy to slack off when you're training alone, talk yourself out of doing that last circuit or that final set of weights. You cheat only yourself.

Going to the very edge of your physical and metal endurance for the first time is hard, reaching the very limits of what you're capable of. It's a dark place, you have to fight the urge to give up, but stay the course because once you've gone there, you can do it again and again, and that gives you a confidence in matches. Not all players can do that. I've seen players give up. They don't walk off the field but the spirit goes out of their bodies, and out of their eyes. But I believe no one has limits, we think we do, we're told we do, but we can always push ourselves further than we believe. Look at the stories we hear in the news about ordinary people suddenly confronted with extraordinary situations who achieve incredible feats of endurance and survival.

I love playing with that line, nudging it back a little further each time. I enjoy being in a really hard situation in a game and feeling comfortable, feeling that all the grunt I've put in on the training park and in the gym is paying off. A great example was the 2010 Top 14 semi-final against Toulon that went to extra-time. Of course it was tough, playing an extra twenty minutes, but at no time did I feel I'd reached the limits of my endurance. I still had gas in the tank and strength in my legs, and most importantly, I had belief in my mind.

Fatigue can turn a player into a coward. You're so tired that you don't bust a gut to make that last-ditch tackle or you don't hit the breakdown the way you should. What I've always believed is that you're only tired when you stop, and that applies to a match or in training. When you're in the thick of the action you don't notice the fatigue; it's only when you stop that you realise you're blowing out of your ass. So the advice I give to young players is keep playing. Focus on keeping your technique right, on your positioning, on making the tackle. And when you've made it, get up and go again. Sure, when you're fatigued you're not moving as fast as you normal but that's OK. Just don't stop.

My desire to push myself to the bottom of my soul is tied to a serious competitive streak. Again, that's always been there. As a kid, whatever I did I wanted to be the best, I wanted to win. The first time I ever appeared in our local newspaper, The Squamish Chief, was in September 1986. There I am, aged eight, on the front page, in natty pair of dungarees, neck and neck with another boy to win a three kilometre running race. I wanted to dominate everything I did and later, as a hit my teens, that singled-mindedness got me into trouble because I wanted to dominate my peers, and if some kid from out of town appeared in Squamish I often ended up fighting him. It was like the old line in the Wild West movies: 'This town ain't big enough for the two of us'.

Later on, as I became an adult, I used to get pretty angry with myself if something didn't go according to plan. I wanted everything to be perfect, to be under my control. I'm much mellower now. If you give 100% but it doesn't work out the way you'd hoped then don't be too disappointed. You gave it your best shot but it wasn't to be. C'est la vie.

Similarly, as I've got older I've found it easier to deal with a slump in form. That's natural, I guess, because experience teaches you how to handle a run of indifferent games. But I still tend to try and just will things to improve. Does that make sense? By that I mean, I grit my teeth, tell myself not to worry, and play myself back into form. My dad gave me a piece of advice a few years ago that I've never forgotten: 'Just keep doing the simple things right and the rest will take of itself'. That certainly is true in rugby because the fatal mistake when you're not playing well is to try too hard to put things right. That will just make it worse. So I go back to basics. I push hard in the scrum, I tackle properly, I secure clean line-out ball and I hit the breakdown hard. I don't look to make fifty metres a game or attempt some risky offload. But ultimately I get through a patch of poor form by working hard, and playing to my strengths that will bring me out the other side.

When I am frustrated with how I'm playing it can be hard for Jennifer. I'm someone who prefers to work through a rugby problem on my own. I don't really bring my work home with me. When I leave the club I switch to dad and husband mode and I don't want to burden her and the kids with my rugby concerns. I'm sure there are times she'd like me to open up more but she married a stubborn guy. Having said that, I married a stubborn girl !

Chapter Eighteen

The 2013-14 season wasn't one of Clermont's finest. Our nemesis, Castres, beat us in the quarter-final of the Top 14, and in the Heineken Cup we were humiliated 46-6 by Saracens in the semi-final. Clermont could point to a couple of controversial refereeing decisions in the first-half that did us no favours, but the truth was we got stuffed good and proper. Saracens were electric and we were awful. We were unable to adapt our game and we just kept running into their back-row off the ruck and never worked out how to combat their rush defence.

In what was the last season of the Heineken Cup, before the tournament was reorganised as the Champions Cup, Saracens ran up forty points in the semi, the first time any club had reached such a figure at that stage of the competition.

It was terrible way for Vern Cotter to leave the club after the eight years of incredible effort he'd put in but in hindsight perhaps it wasn't that surprising that we struggled in the 2013-14 season. After our collapse the previous season, losing the Heineken Cup final against Toulon and then capitulating against Castres, Vern had given a characteristically honest interview with La Montagne, the local paper. He doesn't talk much to the press but when Vern does he doesn't hold back.

He held up his hands and accepted his share of the responsibility for the results but he also bemoaned our game management. He also alluded to the fact some of the squad weren't developing the way he'd hoped, but reserved his biggest criticisms for the men upstairs. He revealed that he was strongly against the decision to loan Viktor Kolelishvili to Lyon for the 2013-14 season, and he also disclosed that Clermont had at one stage been in talks with Jonathan Sexton, the Leinster and

Ireland fly-half. But in the end Sexton went to Racing 92 because they offered twice as much.

Vern was frustrated, too, that the club appeared reluctant to invest in the high performance tools needed to compete with the likes of Toulon and the other top European clubs. In short there was an air of complacency about the people running Clermont that pissed Vern off. It pissed me off, too.

So Vern was right to go public with his concerns about the mismanagement of the club. But of course it didn't go down well within the club. René Fontès, the president, said he was "profoundly disappointed" with Vern's comments and there was a lot of speculation that he would leave the club there and then, instead of staying until the end of the 2013-14 season. He'd already agreed to take up the position as Scotland coach in July 2014 and the players didn't have a problem with him announcing that 12 months early. Better to announce it at the start of the season, so the squad knows where it stands, than leaving it until April or May when it will disrupt the changing-room.

I'm delighted that Vern is returning to France as head coach of Montpellier for the 2017-18 season. He'll do well. He's got a hell of a squad and he'll also have a support structure that he didn't have at Clermont when he was continually butting heads with Jean-Marc. Mohed Altrad, the Montpellier president, is a man who wants to win and has the money to go with his ambition. They've risen far in the last decade and I think the appointment of Vern as head coach could be the missing piece in the jigsaw to take them from also rans to a major power in the European game.

When Vern did leave in the summer of 2014 he was succeeded by Franck Azema, who had been on the Perpignan coaching staff when they beat us in the 2009 Top 14 final, and joined Clermont the following year as backs coach.

To work alongside him Franck hired Jono Gibbes, the former All Black loose forward who had spent six seasons coaching the Leinster forwards. In that time Leinster had won three Heineken Cup titles and within a short time of his arrival it was apparent that Jono was a superb coach and a great guy - and not just because he's married to a Canadian. He's the most precise guy I think I'v ever met. In fact, there may be a bit of Obsessive-Compulsive Disorder in there! Jono is only happy when everything is perfectly lined up. He's great at analysing the game and spotting the little things that when tightened can make big improvements. Jono's been huge for Clermont because he's played at a high level not long ago and he knows that we know how to play rugby, so he doesn't need to overload players with information. Jono wasn't the only new face for the 2014-15 season. Camille Lopez, who had won a couple of caps for France on the tour to New Zealand in 2013, had signed from Perpignan and there were a couple of Brits in Nick Abendanon and Jonathan Davies. Nick, in particular, proved to be a astute signing on the part of the club. He'd been capped by England in 2007 and despite being a consistent performer at full-back for Bath he had been overlooked by Martin Johnson and Stuart Lancaster. By modern standards Nick isn't the biggest but he's got a brain on him. When Clermont sounded him out about a move, before he agreed to anything he studied videos of Top 14 matches and saw that his pace and agility could exploit the holes created by the slower, heavier packs in French rugby. And so it proved. In his first year in France Nick was voted Top 14 Player of the Season by L'Equipe and European Player of the Season by the tournament organisers.

Jonathan Davies, or the Fox, as he was nicknamed, had a less happy time at Clermont. Injuries played a part, and it was a devastating blow for him when he tore his anterior cruciate ligament at the end of the 2014-15 season and was ruled out of Wales' World Cup campaign. But during his two seasons at Clermont Jonathan was also caught in the club v country row, as I had been for many years. If I've one regret in my rugby career it's that I didn't play for Canada between the end of the 2007 World Cup and the warm-up matches for the 2011 tournament. I should have been stronger, but having said that in 2007 Clermont was on the rise and we were becoming a force in France and in Europe. It might well have been detrimental to my career if I had insisted on putting Canada first. If I went to the office to ask if I could be released to play for my country it would either be a flat out 'no' or I'd receive an answer along the lines of 'We've got a string of big matches in that period and we could really do with you'. On one or two occasions they mentioned the 'contract' word. If a Test match fell inside the international window they knew they couldn't stop me going so instead Clermont would mutter something about 'meeting soon to discuss contract extensions and we need to know we can count on players' loyalty'. The message was clear: make a choice between Clermont and Canada. Like I said, I should have perhaps put my foot down, which I did more after 2011 but in those early years I was young and inexperienced. Plus I liked the club, I didn't want to be released.

I wasn't the only one. Jonathan Davies suffered from the same thing, and so did a number of the other boys. Obviously there was no such conflict of interest for the French players. Clermont were only too happy to wave them off to play for Les Bleus. They were proud to have French internationals but if a Canadian, Georgian or Argentine dared ask to be released to represent his country they were usually met with shocked outrage. It was a poor attitude. The reason we were signed by Clermont in the first place was because we were international rugby players. And playing Test match rugby makes you a better player so surely Clermont should have been as pleased for us as they were for their French players.

This goes on at many clubs in Europe. I've heard numerous stories of Pacific Island guys, Georgians or fellow Canadians who have been offered either more money or longer contracts in order to put club before country. It's a horrible dilemma to be in because the life of a professional player is short, and remember, this is our talent, what we're good at in life. Most players' careers are over by their early to mid-thirties, an age when if you're a lawyer, doctor, or businessman you're still considered relatively inexperienced. So players are entitled to cash in while they can and if your club offers you a big financial incentive to turn down your country it's hard to resist.

This is something that happens in other countries as well as France. An example that springs to mind is the Canada flanker Tyler Ardron, a superb player who plays for the Ospreys in Wales.

He suffered a serious knee injury at the 2015 World Cup and battled his way back to fitness by the end of the season. He was sounded out about playing for Canada in

June 2016 but his contract was up for renewal at the Ospreys and he was worried about getting injured in the Tests. I don't blame Tyler for a minute. But the tier one players don't have to deal with the dilemma.

The cases that really piss me off are those like young Cam Pierce down at Pau. Cam is another talented Canadian, who spent a couple of seasons in the Clermont Espoirs before joining Pau. In four seasons with Pau he's played only a handful of matches yet they still hold him back some times from playing for Canada.

*

So in July 2014 there was a new-look to the Clermont squad and there was a feeling that after the disappointments of recent season we had turned a page. Additionally, Jonny Wilkinson had retired at the end of the 2013-14 season, having guided Toulon to a European and domestic double, and there was a belief in the French press that with their talisman gone the champions' had lost their air of invincibility.

On Saturday July 19 we boarded the yellow Clermont bus and headed south for a summer training camp in Falgos, in the Pyrénées-Orientales. As it was a long journey and we had a week of hard training in front of us we stopped for the evening in Millau. It's an isolated town, probably quite fun in the summer with all the outdoor sports on the doorstep but I wouldn't fancy living there in the depths of winter.

On arriving at the hotel we checked in and then held a court session. Most of the boys got fines of some sort and everyone was relaxed and in good spirits. As it was a bonding evening, a chance for the new guys to get to know each other, it seemed only right that we were literally bonded. In groups of three we were strapped to each other, not too bad for the guys on the flanks but not much fun for the one in the middle. The tour rule stated that we weren't allowed to take the straps off until midnight. It was rugby's answer to Cinderella, and there were a few socially awkward moments. Remember the cliche about women also going to the toilets in pairs? Well, imagine what it's like for three guys to go to the toilet strapped to each other...

But it was a good evening and we were welcomed by the locals, some of whom joined our group, and had a few beers with us. At midnight the straps came off and we were free to do what we fancied. I had been tasked with babysitting Jonathan Davies and by midnight the 'Fox' was struggling. So I thought it best if I took him home. In fact I had to carry him back to the hotel and that was no easy task - he's one heavy Welshman.

Quite a few of the boys came with me and once back at the hotel we hit the sack and slept like babies. When we woke in the morning it was to learn that three of the boys were in hospital after being attacked by machete-wielding thugs. Apparently what happened was that a group went to a nightclub and outside the entrance they ran into this group of young men who had just been kicied out of the club. There was a minor altercation and a few words were exchanged. A couple of the Georgian guys were all for sorting it out there and then. But Aurelien Rougerie calmed everyone down and the boys went inside the club. A section of the club had been cordoned off for them but the boys weren't having that; they mingled with the locals and had a great time until the club closed around three in the morning. They left in a group and began walking back to the hotel but there was a sudden summer storm, and that's what split up the boys. Some began running back to the hotel, others took shelter for a few minutes and a few just walked through the rain. And that's when they got ambushed. Around ten punks on scooters appeared, the ones outside the club a few hours earlier, and now they were armed with knives and machetes. Aurelien Rougerie, Julien Pierre and Benjamin Kayser ended up literally fighting for their lives. JP came off the worst, he required an operation after his hip was sliced open, but Roro and Ben both suffered nasty cuts to their arms as they fended off blows. Some of the locals, who bravely came to the players' assistance, were also wounded. It was terrifying and not surprisingly all three were very shaken up. It was incredible that a run-of-the mill exchange of words, the sort of macho posturing that happens in most towns on a Saturday night, escalated into something so serious. The police soon arrested a number of suspects, six of whom are due in court in 2017 accused of armed assault.

Nick Abendanon and Jon Davies must have wondered what the hell they'd let themselves in for! But I'm afraid that wasn't the only fright 'the fox' got during his first season at Clermont. When he arrived in Clermont Jon stayed at Damien Chouly's for a while until he got a place of his own. Damien lived quite close to me so one night I thought it might be fun to play a trick on the new boy. I sometimes went night hunting with a neighbour, shooting foxes who were coming on to his property. Occasionally a couple of boys would come and I think on this occasion Julien Bonnaire and Julien Bardy, Clermont's Portuguese flanker, were along for a night's hunting. We shot a couple of foxes and left them on the doorstep of Damien's house in an amorous embrace. When Jonathan arrived at training the next morning he couldn't wait to tell the squad what he'd found on the doorstep. Of course, Damien knew straight away who was responsible, but he kept quiet leaving the 'Fox' to spend the whole day wondering how the foxes had got there. I would liked to have kept the mystery going a while longer but the look of bemusement on Jon's face made me confess. He took it well. Reasonably well.

We began the 2014-15 season with victories over Grenoble and Bayonne, but in our third match we were beaten 21-20 at home by Montpellier. No longer was the Stade Marcel-Michelin the fortress it once was. The previous May we had lost at home to Castres in the Top 14 quarter-final, bringing to an end 77 consecutive victories in all competitions at the Marcel-Michelin. It was a record that stretched back to November 21 2009 when we had lost 13-9 to Biarritz.

We responded to the Montpellier defeat by winning our next four matches, against Racing, Toulouse, Lyon and Oyonnax, but were then humbled 51-21 at Bordeaux. Franck had decided to rest a number of players, including Damien Chouly, Benjamin Kayser and Thomas Domingo but that was no excuse. There were clearly weaknesses in the squad caused by Clermont's dubious recruitment policy. Nonetheless we finished the season in second place, a point behind Toulon who, while not the force of previous years were still to strong for the likes of Toulouse and Racing. It had been an open championship with no dominant team and the fact

Stade Francais and Oyonnax finished in the top six proved the point. Stade, who had won five league titles between 1998 and 2007, had fallen on hard times subsequently and nearly went bankrupt in 2011. But the Savare family had come to the rescue and the appointment of the intelligent Gonzalo Quesada as head coach had revitalised their fortunes.

Despite qualifying for the play-offs Stade weren't considered serious title contenders but in stunning back-to-back victories they smashed Racing 38-15 and then stunned reigning champions Toulon 33-16 in the semi-final to reach their first Top 14 final since 2007.

Meanwhile Clermont edged past Toulouse 18-14 in a dour semi-final to set up a repeat of the 2007 final. But there would be no opportunity for me to avenge that defeat. I had to watch the final from the stand. Outwardly I looked OK but in fact my health had been seriously compromised by a combination of incompetence and indifference on the part of Clermont.

2015 Champions & Concussion

Clermont were drawn in the proverbial pool of death in Europe, grouped with Saracens, Munster and Sale Sharks. It was the inaugural season of the Champions Cup, with the Heineken Cup having died a death on the battlefield of rugby politics. I take a little bit of interest in politics but not that much. I don't have any say on the decisions made so why fret and fuss?

We began our European campaign away at Saracens, who just a few months earlier had inflicted on Clermont a record 46-6 defeat in the semi-final of the Heineken Cup. We at least gave the English club a game this time but still came out second best, losing 30-23 in a match that showcased European rugby at its finest. It was 10-10 at the break after a first half of bone-shaking intensity. Neither pack was able to exert much in the way of dominance and in the second half as the forwards began to tire so the gaps began to be found. The Saracens' wingers, David Strettle (who would sign for Clermont the following season) and Chris Ashton, both scored a pair of tries, while our winger, Zac Guildford, went over for two tries. One was an absolute gem. Sprinting after a box kick from Ludovic Radosavljevic, Zac leapt high, plucked the ball out of the air, pirouetted and outpaced the Saracens' defence to the try-line,. It showed his class but, alas, the Kiwi was never able to overcome his demons. His struggles to control his drinking had been well documented during the 2011 World Cup and perhaps he thought coming to France would offer him the chance of a fresh start. But within a month of arriving in August 2014 he was involved in a fight in Clermont on a Saturday night and before the season was out Zac had returned to New Zealand.

The contrasting fortunes of Nick Abendanon and Zac shines a light on the whole issue of overseas players in France. Why do some fail and other thrive? Zac had his alcohol problems but the reason why guys like Nick, Brock James, Nathan Hines and myself have made such a good fist of it in France is because we embraced the culture. If you don't then you will be constantly battling everything, complaining about this and that. Accept the fact they do things differently in France. In particular quite a few South Africans have trouble with that. They keep fighting the system but they can fight as hard as they want because they'll never win. The French aren't going to change. So accept it or move on. And try to learn at least some of the language. Don't worry about making an ass of yourself with a wrong word or two. Who cares! Laugh about it, don't be embarrassed.

It was hard, too, for Zac, and Jonathan Davies, that they came out to Clermont as single guys. Players can get lonely in the evenings after training if they go back to an empty flat. Having a wife or girlfriend alleviates that loneliness but it can also, in some cases, be a source of unhappiness. Players come to the club and have a ready-made family. Their partners are stuck at home and again it's up to them: do they want to embrace the culture, make friends with the French wives or do they prefer sitting at home miserable and bored, waiting for their husband to come home from training? Nick and his wife have thrown themselves into the French way of life and they're having a ball.

It's also important to have a good agent. As a breed they are often maligned, sharp suits and sharp tongued, but in my experience most rugby agents are good guys offering sound advice. I worked with Laurent Laffitte for a number of years and he was great. He helped me deal with a lot of things at Clermont when I had discipline problems and was always willing to fight my corner in trying to juggle club and country commitments.

*

The defeat to Saracens was our only reverse in the group stage. We beat Sale home and away, as we did Munster, and that meant the final group game, at home to Saracens, would decide which of us finished top. Unfortunately I failed a fitness test for the game, unable to recover from a knock to my knee in the win against Sale the previous week, and we were also without Aurelien Rougerie, who'd recently undergone an elbow operation.

There was no repeat of the free-flowing rugby of our first clash. It was a tight, dour match, befitting the wintry conditions, and we scored the only try of the match to win 18-6. Our reward for finishing top of the pool was a home quarter-final against Northampton, the English champions.

We destroyed them 37-5. It was one of the most powerful displays from a Clermont side that I could remember. The backs got the headlines with Nick Abendanon, Wesley Fofana and Noa Nakaitacu all scoring classy tries, but the Saints had the soul ripped of out them up front. The Clermont pack was a juggernaut, destroying England's finest, and sending out a message to the rest of Europe: this was our year.

A fortnight later we travelled to the Stade Geoffroy-Guichard in Saint-Etienne for our semi-final. Our opponents were Saracens, who, despite finishing runners-up behind Clermont, had qualified for the quarter-final as one of the pool stage's best losers and then beaten Racing 92 in Paris with the last kick of the game.

I'd played at the Stade Geoffroy-Guichard before, in Clermont's epic extra-time win over Toulon in the 2010 Top-14 semi-final, and in my mind it's one of France's most atmospheric stadiums. Its design is based on the old-style English football grounds with four steep stands that capture the roar of the fans and sends it reverberating around the stadium. From the moment Clermont and Saracens ran our for the semi-final in front of 41,000 fans the atmosphere was electric.

It was pretty red hot out in the middle. There's been little to separate us in the two pool matches and in the first quarter of the match the only points came from the boot of the Saracens fly-half, Charlie Hodgson. Then on 22 minutes I had a head on head with Billy Vunipola in a ruck. It was full-on. Crack. I have a vague recollection of lying on the ground thinking, 'oof, that was a good one'. In the collision I was cut open and I left the field with blood trickling down my forehead. When I got to the touchline the Clermont doctor could see I wasn't well. I wasn't being sick but I was woozy and wasn't seeing straight. The doctor looked me over and said, 'listen, you've had a head knock and we're going to go through the concussion protocol'. He gave me five or six words that I had to repeat. I got just one of them, the last one. By this stage I was doubting myself. I desperately wanted to get back out there but the doctor said, 'No, Jamie, it's finished for you today, you're out'.

I was extremely upset. I wasn't getting aggressive towards the doctor but I was trying to convince him I was good to go. But he took the correct and responsible decision that I wasn't fit to continue. I'd failed the protocol test and that was that. I returned to the changing room and started taking off my boots. A couple of minutes later the doctor appeared at the door. His tone had suddenly altered. 'How do you feel?' he asked. 'Do you feel like you've recovering'. 'Hell, yeah!' I said. 'I'm fine'. So the doctor told me I could go back on the field. I needed no second invitation and ten minutes after the head clash I was back on, packing down in the second row alongside Sébastien Vahaamahina with Julien Pierre back on the bench.

Ask me about the rest of the match and I can't really tell you much. I have a couple of hazy memories, a drive in the Saracens 22 at some point and an attempted tackle right at the end of the match on David Strettle, but I remember little else of the match. But Clermont won, 13-9, so the club was happy. And so was I.

Happy but my head was cloudy. It was still cloudy the next day when I woke up. And the next day. I went into training on the Monday but was **pretty much given the whole week** off. I did a bit of fitness on the bike, had a bit of physio, but generally took it easy. I didn't feel nauseous or have a problem sleeping but my head felt cloudy the whole week and I was a bit slow in everything I did.

I obviously sat out the Top 14 match that weekend but the club made it clear they hoped I would be fit for the Champions Cup final the following Saturday, against our old adversaries Toulon at Twickenham.

On the Monday before the final I was examined by a neurologist. I went through the concussion protocol with him, it was thorough, and I have no complaints, and he passed me. By this stage I was feeling better, or at least I told myself I was feeling better. In much the same way I will myself through patches of bad form, I was willing myself to feel OK. I've always come back quickly from injury so I had a innate sense of self-belief in my powers of recovery. Midway during the week I returned to more strenuous training and believed I was fit for the final, which would also be my fiftieth Champions Cup appearance. I wasn't fit, of course, and on reflection, I knew I wasn't, deep down. I'd talked myself into being fit, encouraged by the club. I take some of the blame for that, but what unfolded at Twickenham was all Clermont's fault.

Clermont had to make a late change on the day of the final when Brock James injured his thigh in the warm-up. Camille Lopez was promoted from the bench to fly-half and he got the first points on the board with a penalty on seven minutes. Three minutes later my meaningful participation in the match ended. I remember lining up the Toulon hooker, Guilhem Guirado, but as I positioned myself for the tackle my old buddy Chris Masoe got in the way of his Toulon teammate. So I actually tackled him. I hit him with my shoulder, not my head, it was a text-book tackle, but the shock of the impact was enough to knock me out. If you watch the TV pictures I'm gone the moment I make contact with Masoe.

I walked off unaided, and compared to the semi-final I didn't look too bad. But that's the whole point. The real damage was done against Saracens. Running into Masoe was a secondary concussion that simply exacerbated the trauma of the initial blow. My dad had flown over for the final and he and Jennifer were sitting together in the stands. When they saw me come off they presumed my final was over. When I returned to the pitch six minutes later Jennifer was distraught. She knew I wasn't fit and she watched the rest of the game beside herself with worry. My dad was obviously concerned, picking up on Jennifer's distress, but he hadn't seen me in the days after the semi-final. And being a doctor himself, he trusted the medical staff. If I was allowed to return then surely I was fit. Wasn't I?

No. Twelve minutes into the second half I attempted to tackle the Toulon flanker, Juan Smith, but the collision left me dazed and groggy. There was also a cut to my head so I went off to have that treated. As I sat in the changing room I threw up. I was in a hell in a state, to be honest, and incapable of making any rational decision. But I wanted to carry on playing so back out I went for the last 13 minutes of the match. By this time Jennifer could not believe what was going on, and my dad too could see I wasn't right.

I finished the match - I actually remember more about the final than I do the semi-final because the concussion at Twickenham was secondary - and the decisive try from Drew Mitchell that won Toulon the game was superb. It was another defeat for Clermont, an all-too familiar tale, but in the days and weeks after the final I was more concerned with my health than than of Clermont's.

I think it affected Jennifer the most. She told me subsequently that she was practically having a panic attack when I came out for the second time, and she's never forgiven Clermont for the way they handled the situation.

Let's be frank about this, Clermont gambled with my health in their pursuit of glory, and they're not the only club to have put success before the well-being of players. If I'd suffered a similar injury playing for the Capilanos or Llandovery I would have come off and never gone back on. That's because those clubs are amateur and what matters to them are the players. That's not the case at the top end of the professional game. Players are lumps of meat with a limited life span so, hell, the clubs are going to work them into the ground. We're beasts of burden. We're useful so long as we perform and the clubs will do anything to make us perform because the better the performance the bigger the profit. What matters to clubs are winning trophies, reaching play-offs, avoiding relegation. That's what makes the 'suits' happy, it means they can bask in the reflected glory. The players? We come and go. There'll always be a steady stream of bright young things ready to put their bodies on the line in the belief they're really valued by the club. Don't get me wrong, there are some fine people who work behind the scenes at Clermont and other clubs, but the bottom line these days is it's all about the balance sheet and the trophy cabinet. Me and every other player know the risks when we sign a professional contract and we're aware it's an intensely physically sport with an element of danger. But at the same time we need to feel we'll be looked after if we do take one for the team. And above all, it's imperative we know our long-term health won't be played like a roulette wheel.

Clermont have two team doctors and it was a different one for the final than the semi-final. So neither covered himself in glory. I asked the one at Twickenham why, having seen me puke into a garbage can, he allowed to go back out. Vomiting is one of the symptoms of concussion. He said 'Oh, I wasn't sure if it was just the tension of the match making you sick. I've seen lot of players throw up because of pressure'. Maybe he has, but he's never seen me because I've never been sick because of tension. So for the doctor to say that was a complete cop out.

I also asked the doctor on duty at Saint-Etienne why he changed his mind in the space of a couple of minutes. One moment my day was done, and the next I was being told to get back out there because Sébastien Vahaamahina was struggling - by the way, if he was struggling, he recovered because when I came back on for the semi it was for Julien Pierre, the substitute. All the doctor said was I was fit to continue. In other words he changed his story after the match. I'll let others decide if those two doctors acted ethically. I don't bear them any ill-will. They were weak under pressure from above. During the Saint Etienne game something, or more accurately, someone, made the doctor revise his opinion about my health. I don't know if a message was sent from the staff, from the manager, whoever, but he definitely changed his mind.

I have no complaints about the treatment I received after the match. I had a battery of blood tests and was sent to see one of the best **neurosurgeon in France. Perhaps Clermont felt guilty? But the damage had already been done. The club was being reactive when they needed to be pro-active.**

It's an issue I've spoken about at length with my dad, getting his view as both a former player of some repute but more significantly as a doctor of huge experience. Regarding my own experience he was furious when he discovered what had happened. 'Unconscionable' was the word he used to describe the doctor's decision to let me return to the field after I'd been sick.

When he was playing he never got concussed and he can't remember any teammate or opponent who was. Obviously players got a bang on the head but forty years ago the players were half the size and weight of today's professionals. The collisions were minuscule compared to today's hit. But the problem is that in France they're attitude to concussion is stuck in the 1970s. Never was this more evident than in the 2014 Top Final quarter-final between Toulouse and Racing. Midway during the first half Toulouse centre Florian Fritz took a terrible blow to the head in an accidental collision with Racing lock Francois Van der Merwe. Blood pumped from Fritz's head and it was clear from his vacant stare as he was led from the field that he didn't know who he was or where he was.

Minutes later television pictures showed Toulouse coach Guy Noves at the door of the Toulouse dressing room, urging the medical staff to hurry in their work because the 15 minute blood injury time limit was nearly up. Fritz, as all of us would do in his place, didn't want to let his team down, so he staggered back out to the general horror of his teammates. "I had a small KO," he said later. "I don't remember everything."

Noves was hammered by the press and the public yet was he contrite? The opposite. He didn't understand what all the fuss was about. "I have been knocked out, played on and was fine," he told reporters. "As you can see, I am still standing here".

Noves is the same generation as my dad. When he played for France in the 1970s he weighed 78 kilos, a couple of kilos lighter than his captain Jean-Pierre Rives. Rives was a flanker. Can you imagine France fielding a flanker in 2017 who was 80 kilos?

Same goes for the great scrum-half of that era Jacques Fouroux, who stood 1m 62cm and weighed 65kgs.

Rugby has changed, and the only flanker you're likely to see weighing 80kgs will be on a school rugby field. Last time I asked, Damien Chouly weighed in at 110kgs. Yet despite the transformation in physiques and the simultaneous increases in pace and power, attitudes to concussion are only now catching up - a good twenty years too late. Any one who played rugby up until the start of the 21st century can tell you what the cure was for a bang on the head - the magic sponge. Only it wasn't magic, was it, it was cold, dirty and soaked in the blood of your teammates. Even up to a few years ago there was no proper procedure in place in France. I got clattered by Henry Tuilagi during the 2010 Top 14 Final. Any time one of those big Samoan boys hit you, you know about it and I was down and out for a few moments. There was no Head Injury Assessment at that time so my treatment consisted of having the contents of a water bottle poured over my head. I finished the game (which Tuilagi didn't!) but that was because of my own bloody-mindedness rather than a bottle of water.

The Ligue Nationale de Rugby [LNR] conducted a three year study into concussion in the Top 14 between the start of the 2012/13 season and the end of the 2014/15 championship and there were on average two cases each weekend. They have the stats so let's act. The figures in amateur rugby in France are even more alarming, as described by *Midi Olympique* in an edition at the start of the season. In the 2015-16 season there were a reported 1,4000 cases of concussion in the amateur ranks, yet for these players there is no procedure to treat injured players. It's deeply disturbing.

First and foremost it's a question of education. Certain coaches need to be better educated in understanding concussion and injuries in general. Last year, while I was still at Clermont, our physiotherapist addressed the squad about how to react on the field if we see a player knocked out. It was interesting because a lot of the guys thought the first thing to do was roll him into the safety position and check he hasn't swallowed his tongue. No. Leave him alone, don't touch him. Let the professional medics do that because if the player's got a neck injury and he's rolled over it could mean he spends the rest of his life in a wheelchair.

So that was an education for some of the Clermont players, and well done for the club in organising that lecture. This is what needs to be done throughout the rugby-playing world, educate players and coaches.

It's something I do increasingly as I spend more time coaching. In February last year I spent some time coaching the national squad back in Canada. In one game one of our players got a nasty head knock and straight away I brought him off. He wasn't happy. He thought he was still fit and could keep playing, and he told me so in no uncertain terms. I said 'listen, I've gone through it. You're a rugby player you want to play but you don't play with a bum knee, do you? Because if you do you know it could get worse. Exactly the same with a head knock. You don't know how serious the injury is so it's better to err on the side of caution'.

If you break a hand or tear your knee ligaments it's a physical injury. You can see you're injured and so can the rest of the squad. But with concussion you often look outwardly OK. Sure, like I did after the semi-final, you might feel cloudy but you're not hobbling around with bits of you in plaster. It takes courage to go the team doctor and say 'you know what, I don't think feel quite right'. No one wants to be accused of malingering and rugby is founded on being a sport for tough, strong men and women. Play through the pain, we've all heard that expression. But playing through the pain could result in you enduring a lifetime of pain.

I know it's hard for some guys, particularly younger guys making their way at a club, to say they're not feeling right. The temptation is to keep playing, to earn a reputation for being a great team guy who never lets the club down. But by playing on through a concussion you're letting everyone down and ultimately you could be putting your life on the line.

Chapter Nineteen

If my wife suffered at Twickenham the worst was yet to come for Jennifer. When we first met in 2006 she had no idea how big rugby was in France. She thought it was like Canada, a sport played in in front of a few hundred people, a thousand on a good day. The first time that I took Jennifer to the Stade Marcel Michelin I was injured, and so we sat together in the stands. As we took our seats the fans were chanting my name and waving. She was shocked and from that day on rugby has taken over her life and she's experienced the ups and downs every step of the way with me.

My fight with Paul O'Connell, for example, she watched on TV back in Clermont. She'd invited a group of the players' wives and girlfriends over for Sunday lunch and then they watched the match together. When the fight started Jennifer was screaming at the TV. I've never actually asked if she was screaming at me to stop hitting Paul or for Paul to stop hitting me. Perhaps some questions are best left unasked!

As the relationship developed and I went from being boyfriend to husband to father the stress for Jennifer has increased. So has the incursion of rugby into our day to day lives. Playing for Clermont there were no 'days-off' for me. Because of my size I stand out wherever I go, and in a rugby-mad place like Clermont that meant I was always visible out and about. As I've said I found overwhelmingly that the people were courteous and respectful, and recognised that there is a time and a place for an autograph, a selfie or just a hello and handshake. Nonetheless even when we went to a restaurant there would be glances or nudges, and a whispered 'look, it's Jamie'. On occasions it felt like even though we were left alone we were exhibits in a zoo.

It happens all over France and in fact all over the world. A few years ago we managed, just the two of us, to grab a few days vacation in Dubai. At one moment a local woman in a headscarf approached Jennifer and asked if I was a Mixed Martial Arts fighter. I was standing right there but of course she wouldn't address the question directly to me so Jennifer replied that I was a rugby player. She looked a little disappointed.

At other times being recognised has led to commercial opportunities. We were dining together in a London restaurant during the 2015 World Cup and the family on the nearest table were rugby fans. They said hello, we started talking, and by the end of the evening we'd agreed a deal to wear their company's shoes. So it pays to be friendly.

But I wasn't that friendly in the weeks following my concussion. For a start Clermont blew another Top 14 final - their eleventh - when they lost 12-6 to Stade Francais. I watched from the sidelines and in my opinion that was our worst defeat of the ones I'd seen. With the greatest respect to Stade they weren't a patch on the side that had beaten us in 2007, nor were they worthy of comparison to Toulouse in 2008 or Perpignan in 2009. They were a workmanlike side, who did the basics well, and on the night played with greater precision that Clermont and kept their heads under pressure.

So ended another season without silverware for Clermont and the squad went their separate ways for the summer. For many of us the focus switched to the impending World Cup but I was still unsure whether I'd be passed fit to play in my fourth tournament.

I was like the proverbial bear with the sore head throughout June and into early July. I suffered headaches, mood swings and insomnia. I felt lethargic and run down much of the time but when I tried to sleep I couldn't. I was reduced to lying on my couch doing nothing . I would snap at Jennifer, even snap at the kids if they made too much noise. I hated the whole situation and it was scary to feel **my personality had changed. In order not to worry Jennifer I tried to put up this front that everything was OK but she knew of course it wasn't. She became angry at me for putting up the front and so we would argue. I remember one time she said 'wouldn't it be lovely it you had a regular job and we had a regular life so we could live like a regular family'. Eventually I emerged from the dark tunnel and was passed fit for the World Cup, joining Gareth Rees, Rod Snow, Mike James, Dave Lougheed and Al Charron as the only Canadians to appear in four tournaments. I'd missed the Pacific Nations Cup matches in the summer against Japan, Tonga and Samoa but captained the side in a warm-up match against a physical Georgia side at Esher, in Surrey. There were some new faces in Canada team and I was truly the old man of the side. I packed down alongside Brett Beukeboom in the second row, who's twelve years my junior, while I had sixteen years on our prop, Djustice Sears-Duru. Amazing to think I'd already been banged up in a couple of juvenile prisons before he'd even been born! Tyler Ardron was coach Kieran Crowley's original choice as captain but he'd injured his knee in the Pacific Nations defeat to Samoa at the end of July and was clearly not going to be fit for our World Cup opener against Ireland in Cardiff. Kieran asked me to fill in and so in my fourth World Cup I led Canada for the first time.**

It was a magnificent occasion at the Millennium Stadium but Ireland were too strong for us. We were under pressure from the start and on 16 minutes I was yellow

carded for being on the wrong side of the ruck metres from our try-line. The referee said I was trying to slow up Irish ball, and I probably was. I called out a few instructions to the boys as I trooped off but in my absence Ireland scored fourteen unanswered points. At half-time they were 29-0 up and the game was over as a contest. We stuck to our task well in the second-half, and played some good rugby in patches, including a try for DTH Van der Merwe. The only consolation I could take from the final score of 50-7 was that my old sparring partner, Paul O'Connell, had also received a yellow card. It goes without saying that his card was more deserved than mine! We had a good laugh about that after the match over a beer, and in the light of the terrible injury he suffered a few weeks later it's a good final memory to have of locking horns with the jolly Green giant.

After Ireland we travelled north to Leeds to play Italy. It was a game we should have won but we lost 23-18 despite playing some of the most attractive rugby I've seen from a Canada side. What we missed was execution in the red zone. Three or four times in the opening half an hour we got into Italy's 22 but we couldn't convert the pressure into tries. That was a reflection on the fact that several members of the squad had come through the Sevens programme and were very good footballers but they lacked the experience of 15s and made decisions that were Sevens decisions. A case in point was in the last quarter of the Romania match when we won a penalty on their scrum. Our scrum-half decided to take a quick penalty and he took off down the short side. The move broke down and Romania cleared the danger, eventually winning 17-15

 The guys have to understand that in a game like that, when you're ahead, you kick for the corners and close out the game. You don't need to play quickly but that's how they do it with their clubs back in Canada or on the Sevens circuit, and when a player is under pressure he reacts by doing what he's comfortable with.

Sandwiched between the Italy and Romania matches was the clash against France in Milton Keynes. Tyler Ardron was back for that match so as I wasn't skipper I had a licence to be mischievous. The opportunity came a few minutes before half-time when the French had a line-out ten metres from our try-line. I saw my buddy

Damien Chouly talking to his pack in a huddle and thought I'd go and say hello, see if he had anything interesting to say. He usually doesn't! As I joined the huddle Eddy Ben Arous, the France prop, glanced at me but he didn't seem that surprised. It was Rabah Slimani who took exception, pushing me back towards my own boys.

If that was my funniest memory from my four World Cups my fondest is harder to pin down. Obviously my first match stands out, against Wales at Melbourne in 2003, and captaining Canada against Ireland in 2015 was special. So too was our 25-20 win over Tonga in the 2011 World Cup

It's highly unlikely I'll join Samoa's Brian Lima as the only player to have appeared in five World Cups. If I did make it to Japan for the 2019 tournament I'd be 41, older than Diego Ormaechea, who holds the record for being the crinkliest player to appear in a World Cup when he played for Uruguay in the 1999 World Cup aged 40 years and 26. I wouldn't mind being a record holder so perhaps I will keep going. Obviously don't tell the wife...

*

The 2015 Rugby World Cup in England was incredibly well run. I can't praise enough the volunteers, the training facilities, the transport and hotels, and of course the crowds with every match sold out. Even the weather was awesome. Here comes the 'but'.

But for what was billed as an extraordinarily friendly and sociable World Cup which it was, it was pretty cheap that we were told to clear off within 24 hours of our final match against Romania. I vented my anger on twitter, and got a swift response from Brett Gosper, the chief executive of World Rugby. I didn't want to become embroiled in a spat on social media, and nor did I wish to appear churlish and petty, so I let the matter lie, but I'll revisit it now briefly.

The problem, and it affects all the tier two countries, those nations on the periphery of world rugby, is that the players and the backroom staff work so hard, and sacrifice so much, to get to a World Cup. Some of these guys are amateur or barely professional and the World Cup is a huge deal for them, more so than the tier one guys who are on a different level financially and in terms of how they're looked after. When Canada played its final match on the Tuesday against Romania most of the guys wanted to hang around for a few days and soak up the atmosphere. Use our players' passes to go to a game or two, and just enjoy the tournament until the following weekend when they would head home. They didn't expect to have their accommodation paid for but they wanted to be able to change their flights to a later date. After all, the players are the main actors in the World Cup. Without us they'd be no show. Instead we were made to feel unwelcome. We had served our purpose, we were no longer actively involved in the rugby, so thank you and goodbye.

I was infuriated at what I saw as petty and mean-spirited bureaucracy, and hence the tweet I sent on the morning of October 7th:

"Thanks @rugbyworldcup for a great tournament! Too bad we have to pay to leave !"

Daniel Leo, the former Samoan player, who's never been shy of speaking his mind, was one of the first to react to the tweet, saying:

"Results aside, @rugbyworldcup has been a shocker for Tier2 sides. Commercially, Scheduling-wise and judicially @WorldRugby found wanting."

To which I replied:

"Hope you guys haven't had to pay to get home like some of us !"

As you imagine that sent social media into overdrive. David Flatman, the former England prop turned astute rugby TV commentator, tweeted:

"Are you kidding me Jamie??? "

If only, David.

Gosper felt compelled to come to the defence of the tournament organisers, tweeting:

"Jamie, you're well aware that it is incorrect to suggest that RWC does not pay return travel."

Like I said twitter isn't really the right forum to have an in-depth discussion about such an important issue so I took it no further. In one sense Brett was right, the

RWC organisers do pay return travel but it has to be within 24 hours. The contentious issue for me was that in my previous three World Cups players did have the option of changing airline tickets for a small fee. That wasn't the case in 2015. I subsequently investigated why this was and apparently somebody in the Canada Rugby Union signed off the travel agreement stipulations without consulting the players. I don't why they did that, whether they didn't read the small print or didn't think it would become an issue.

The first the squad heard about this rule was in the last week of the tournament when we were told we had to leave within 24 hours of our last game or forfeit our tickets home. I obviously wasn't flying back to Canada but I needed to get back to Clermont. The RWC organisers were happy to pay for me to fly from London to Paris and from Paris to Clermont but they wouldn't stump up 300 bucks for the gas that would get me and my family back to France in our car. I tried to explain to them that it didn't make sense, that my way was cheaper than two airline tickets, but rules were rules and there would be no exceptions.

So instead of hanging out together as a squad for a few days after the tournament, quite a few of the boys left the hotel on the Wednesday, took the bus to London and flew back to Canada. One or two of them were carrying injuries and I'm not sure a long-haul flight is advisable for people not 100 per cent healthy.

But that's the World Cup now, it's a business first and foremost for the organisers and to hell with the players. Not long after the 2015 tournament finished Gosper was bragging about the fact the commercial value had increased by 50% on 2011. Good for you, Brett, but perhaps spare more of a thought for the players in 2019.

I ended up out pocket after the 2011 and 2015 tournaments, and so did a lot of the Tier Two players. Now I'm not complaining, because I wouldn't have missed those experiences for the world, but playing in a World Cup can be an expensive business for some of us. In 2011 in New Zealand I bought Jennifer and Maelle over and we paid for that ourselves. Obviously that was our decision but it would have been tough on Jennifer, to leave her in France for four or five weeks with a one-year-old. Rugby Canada do their best to look after us financially during World Cups, and it's certainly improved since the 2003 tournament. From what I recall, we got $275 Canadian dollars per week, which is about €175. At the 2007 World Cup in France we got nothing, at least the professional players in the Canada squad didn't. Money was tight at the time and the pro players waived our payment so the amateurs guys in the squad would be better recompensed for their time and efforts

Every World Cup represents a financial challenge for Canada, and most Tier Two nations. In the build up to the 2015 tournament we appointed Al Charron as a fund-raising co-ordinator and he did a sterling job in boosting Canada's coffers. Nearly €100,000 was raised in 2014 alone, money which was used to assist Canada-based domestic players in their training. World Rugby does contribute - every country that appears in the World received $300,000 (€200 000) - but while that figures looks a lot on paper, in reality it's not.

The crazy thing is that during a World Cup year World Rugby compensates the Tier One nations because there are no Test matches in June and November. So France, England, New Zealand and the rest receive $15 million (€10m) on top of the $300,000 they get for appearing in the World Cup. What Canada could do with $15 million.

It's unfair that the financial pie is distributed so unevenly, particularly when the likes of England and France are plump with revenue already. In the 2015 World Cup each member of the Canada squad received $4,000 (€2,700) over the duration of the tournament. Obviously we had all our food and accommodation paid for, as well as receiving $50 a day.

Compare that to England who, according to a report in the Daily Telegraph on the eve of the 2015 World Cup, shared a combined match fee of £345,000 for each pool game - which works out at £15,000 per player per game. That was more than twice that paid to any other country. The £15,000 comprised a £7,000 match fee, £7,000 for image rights and a £1,000 training fee.

I don't begrudge the English boys that money for a moment. I'm simply highlighting the fact that there is a huge discrepancy at World Cups between the haves and the have-nots, and more needs to be done by World Rugby to bridge this gulf. Every player who plays in a World Cup, whether they're an All Black, a Canadian or a Namibian, has made the same sacrifices to get their and has put their body through the same extreme punishment in order to be selected.

As results at the 2015 World Cup showed the gap in competitiveness is closing. Japan beat South Africa, Canada came within a whisker of beating Italy and Samoa lost by just three points to Scotland. There were a couple of horribly one-sided matches - Uruguay leaked 60 points to England and Australia, and France were hammered 62-13 by the All Blacks (had to slip that in!) - but nothing like the thrashings of previous tournaments.

In the 2003 World Cup, for instance, Australia destroyed Namibia 142-0, England beat Georgia 84-6 and slaughtered Uruguay 111-13, and New Zealand put 90 points past Tonga. No one wants to see matches like those, games that are little more than a training run for the victors, and the record number of spectators - 2.47 million tickets were sold - who attended the 2015 World Cup were treated to the most competitive group stage in the tournament's history.

The end result was that £250 million was generated in ticket revenues, delivering an £80 million surplus to World Rugby. No wonder the organisation's chairman, Bernard Lapasset was happy afterwards. "Rugby World Cup 2015 will be remembered as the biggest tournament to date, but I also believe that it will be remembered as the best," he said in a statement. "England 2015 has been the most competitive, best-attended, most-watched, most socially-engaged, most commercially-successful Rugby World Cup. But this special Rugby World Cup has been about much more than numbers, it has been about the amazing atmosphere in full and vibrant stadia, the excitement around the host nation and in Cardiff, the unforgettable moments played out by the world's best players and the friendships that have been created along the way – the very best of our sport has been on display."

I agree with those sentiments, and I hope as I speak some of that £80m surplus is being ploughed into the Tier Two nations so we become even more competitive in the 2019 World Cup.

By and large I think World Rugby do a good job overseeing the global expansion of the game. It's not their fault that it took the All Blacks until 2015 to finally play a Test match in Samoa having spent the previous half a century pillaging some of their best players. Perhaps Australia will follow suit one day. The European nations are much better at touring the Tier Two nations than the Big Three of the southern hemisphere, particularly Scotland, who first played a Test in Fiji in 1998 and four years later played Tests in Canada and the USA, before touring the Pacific Islands in 2012.

These matches are vital, not just for giving the Tier Two players experience of playing the best sides in the world, but in promoting the sport. I think back to when I played for Canada West v Scotland on that 2002 tour. It was a huge moment for me in my development, the chance to Test myself against the likes of Stuart Grimes and Gordon Bulloch as well as playing in front of nearly 4,000 fans.

Sure, I've been on the receiving end of a couple of thrashings playing for Canada, notably the 70-0 defeat to England at Twickenham in 2004. It stinks to lose like that, and collectively there are few positives take. But individually you learn and improve. That England team had won the World Cup 12 months previously and to play against Jason Robinson, Mike Tindall, Lewis Moody and Steve Thompson was a superb learning experience for me - even if I did only last about 25 minutes. Charlie Hodgson, who was playing fly-half that day for England, kicked off and his kick was perfectly weighted. I jumped up, caught the ball, and as I landed Moody clattered into my leading leg. It was a legitimate hit, and a hard one, but like I said, it's all part of the experience of playing the top sides.

Canada needs regular matches against the top nations if we';re to keep improving. In the summer of 2016 I captained the side in home Tests against Japan, Russia and Italy, all of which drew in good crowds and produced high-quality rugby. Ten thousand fans turned up in Vancouver to watch us play Japan, and we had a crowd of over 13,000 for the Test in Toronto against Italy. Compare those numbers to when I played for Canada against the USA in Vancouver in 2003 - only 3,200 fans. That's a great increase and proof that rugby in Canada is on the up.

The biggest thing that has helped Canada is the globalisation of ideas and knowledge. We now have coaches from Europe bringing their savoir-faire in both 15s and 7s and so the rugby world is much smaller than it was twenty years ago. There are lots of southern hemisphere coaches in Europe - in fact during the 2017 Six Nations only France had a home-grown head coach - and the Fiji squad that won gold in the Olympics Sevens last years was coached by an Englishman. This globalisation of rugby is hugely beneficial for the Tier Two countries as we now have access to ideas and expertise that we didn't in the past.

Rugby in Canada has definitely made a lot of progress in the last fifteen years. More and more kids are playing at high school and those are opportunities that I never had. If we'd had kids coming through in 1991, like we do now, we'd be a lot closer to the top countries. But we're seeing improvements and the Canada U20 team reached the World Trophy Final in 2015. We've got the athletes in Canada, we've just got to get them playing rugby from a younger age. But the rise of Sevens is going to play a part in that, and the Canadian women winning a bronze in the 2016 Olympic Sevens was monumental. It's impossible to emphasize just how big a deal that was in Canada, and how because of the media interest that followed, masses of kids now know about rugby.

Rugby in North America is going to keep growing in the next decade, in the same way soccer has States. The North American market has huge potential and the European clubs are waking up to the fact. Saracens played London Irish in New Jersey in a Premiership match last year, and the European champions have signed up Seattle Saracens to their global network. Now the Top 14 clubs are getting in on the act. Racing 92 have teamed up with Austin Huns, a semi-pro team in the Red River Rugby Conference, and Toulon are doing something similar with Miami. Mourad Boudjellal has his eyes on the recently-formed Pro Rugby championship, which at the moments comprises five franchises: San Francisco, Sacramento, Denver, Ohio and San Diego. I hope Canada will soon join the championship and help it grow into a truly North American league.

The coverage that rugby received during the Olympics was huge in North America, and while it was Sevens and not 15s, it still introduced millions of people to the sport. I'm pretty sure that we'll soon see more and more European and southern hemisphere players heading to the States, the way we do in the Major League Soccer with guys like David Beckham, Frank Lampard , Thierry Henry and Andrea Pirlo finishing their careers with a lucrative contract in the States. I will come a bit too late for me but I would have loved to end my career playing professionally in North America.

<u>Chapter Twenty</u>

I did eventually make it back to Clermont from the World Cup, and the nine months that followed were my most turbulent at the club. I had a good idea that this would be my last season at Clermont. The president, Eric **de Cromières, had intimated in 2014 that at my age it was unlikely they would present me with a new deal, certainly nothing more than a one-year extension, which offers little of the way of job security for someone looking to support a young family. So I started to put out some feelers and received interest from Lyon and Oyonnax, as well as a couple of clubs in England. When I returned from the World Cup it was evident there were one or two people within the club who wanted me out. I was in discussions with my lawyer about starting legal proceedings against Clermont for the way they'd handled my concussion the previous season. That earned me no brownie points but in truth I'd been rubbing some people up the wrong way for a number of seasons because I dared speak my mind. This was particularly true with Jean-Marc Lhermet. I've been playing senior rugby for twenty years and in all that time there are only two people I've actively disliked. The first is Remy Martin, for reasons I've explained, and the second was Lhermet. The guy is a drain on Clermont. From what people tell me he was a good player in his day but in my time at the club he was a pain in the ass. I blame him for making it difficult for me to play for Canada between 2007 and 2011, and he was a constant thorn in the side of Vern Cotter. His job title at the club** was Sporting Director but he couldn't direct a dog to its kennel. Fortunately he's been moved upstairs now, to some vague undefined role, and Franck Azema has assumed his responsibilities. Not that I was aware Lhermet had any responsibilities. When Clermont announced last summer that Lhermet was leaving his post, there was a comment in the paper from Jean-Marc saying that some people at the club felt an "incomprehension at my position". Yes, many of us couldn't comprehend how he got a whack load of money for doing nothing.

My first start for Clermont in the 2015-16 season was the 42-13 win over Castres at the Marcel-Michelin on October 31 and I played throughout the next few weeks. But with each game the pain in my neck grew worse. I'd first had a problem a year earlier when I began suffering contractions in my left trapezius, the muscle that stretches over the back of the neck and shoulders and moves the head and shoulder blade. I'd had an op on my left shoulder in 2010 and I presumed it was connected to that. The pain got worse in December to the point that when we sat down as a family for Christmas dinner I had to cut up and then eat my food with my right hand because my left arm was so painful. Sleeping had become excruciating and I had to put my arm above my head or on a pillow next to me. I would fall asleep and then wake up screaming because of the nerve pain.

I knew I had to address the problem after the match against Racing 92 on December 27. We lost at home 20-16 and I hadn't played well. I'd missed two tackles that normally I would nail. Franck Azema could see something wasn't right and subbed me for Paul Jedrasiak on 55 minutes. "Are you all right?" he asked, as I came off. I told Franck the truth, that I was playing scared because I was worried about my neck. The next day I underwent an MRI scan and that revealed a really big hernia that was starting to push on my spinal column. Two weeks later I had surgery and when I woke up the day after the operation I felt weird. Weird and good. The pain that I'd been living with for more than a year was gone. It felt like I'd undergone some sort of miracle. It took me a few days to realise that I no longer had to protect my left arm doing everyday tasks.

I've detailed my criticisms of Clermont concerning my concussion but I've nothing but praise for the club in how they've looked after my other injuries, the more visible and obvious ones. Which goes back to what I was saying about the need in rugby to educate everyone about concussion. There may not be broken bones or blood but the damage is there, it's hidden.

Considering the number of years I've been playing professional rugby I've been very lucky with injuries. I've haven't suffered any knee or ankle injuries, which are often the ones that end careers. Or is it luck? It's interesting that the players who often enjoy the longest careers are second rows. I'm still going, so is Thibaut Privat, Arnaud Mela, Pascal Pape, Rodrigo Capo Ortega, Ali Williams and Donncha O'Callaghan, all guys in their late thirties,. Then there's the granddaddy of us all, Brad Thorn, who this season came out of retirement to play for Queensland Country in Australia's

National Rugby Championship at the grand old age of 41.

Is is luck or is it to do with the fact that we've bodies that are built for rugby? Or frames are made for carrying a lot of kilos. Of course we bulk up and add on some muscle but not in the same way as some of the backs. You see a lot of backs who have put on so much weight that their frames can't cope and that's why the ankles or knees go. I remember a few years that Gavin Henson, the Wales centre, took a year out from the game. In that time his weight dropped from 92kgs to 69. That's an unhealthy differential in my opinion, and shows that when he was playing his joints were required to carry a considerable increase in weight. My weight has always been around 118kg, maybe a couple of kgs either side, but certainly nothing more than 5kg.

The number of players forced into early retirement is alarming and a sign that the physicality of the game is taking an increasing toll. You could argue that front-rows are built for rugby in the same way as us locks but it doesn't matter how muscular and heavy you are, the forces being applied at scrum-time in the front row are now so massive that more and more props are retiring with neck, back and knee problems.

The worst injuries I've suffered were the torn eyeball when I was gouged playing for

Grenoble against Agen in my first season in France, and then also the knee I took in the face when I was clearing out a ruck in a Top 14 match in the 2008-09 season. I'd fractured something called a plancer orbital (I never even knew I had one of those!) and needed a titanium plate inserted in my face. Then there are the stitches. Don't ask how many. I lost count long ago. I just thank God I've still got a full head of hair because if I went bald my scalp would resemble a railway junction.

Stitches and plates in your face are O.K because they don't affect you in day-to-day life. When I had the neck op I was immobile in bed for ten days and after the shoulder reconstruction in 2010 I only had the use of one arm for a while. Maelle had just been born so that was terribly frustrating. I couldn't cuddle her properly or change her diapers or do a lot of 'dad things'.

When I had the neck operation Maelle was five and Grayson three, ages when kids like to jump on their daddies. I had to ask them to be careful with dad's neck, explaining it in kid's terms, and they were excellent at treating me gently. I got ambushed by Grayson a couple of time but managed to get out of the way in time.

*

My appearances in the 2015-16 Champions Cup were restricted to just two matches. The first was against the Ospreys in the pool opener, a match we won 34-29 to extend our winning European record at the Marcel-Michelin to 24 matches. It was now eight years since we had last lost at home in the competition and the club felt confident of enjoying another good Champions Cup campaign. I was rested for the trip to Exeter and was as dismayed as the fans when we went down 31-14 at Sandy Park. I played in the re-match the following month in what would be my last European game for Clermont and my final appearance in the Champions Cup, thirteen years after coming on for the Scarlets against Glasgow.

It was a satisfying way to bow out, playing my part in a five-try thrashing of Exeter that got our European campaign back on track. We player Bordeaux away in the next game but then lost on the road to the Ospreys. It was a sloppy performance and an undisciplined one, and we had only ourselves to blame for squandering a seven-point lead to lose 21-13.

Normally a side who loses two matches in the Champions Cup pool stage is finished but Clermont were lucky. Results elsewhere had conspired to make us favourites to qualify from the final round of matches, and all we had to do was beat Bordeaux at home to finish top. Even if the unthinkable happened and we lost - but, hey, that was unthinkable, wasn't it, after 25 wins on the bounce?! - a losing bonus point would still see us qualify for the quarter-finals.

But it was clear from the first five minutes that we wouldn't lose. Tries from Jonathan Davies and Noa Nakaitaci put us 14-0 up. Bordeaux were dead and buried. Or that's what we assumed. What unfolded in the next hour was incredible. Great entertainment for the neutral but agony for everyone concerned with Clermont.

Bordeaux scored two tries of their own and a penalty on the stroke of half-time put them 17-14 up at the break. They then extended their lead with another three points early in the second-half. I was watching the game at home, trying not to shout too much for fear of damaging my neck. My nerves were calmed by two Clermont tries in quick succession. Order restored. We were now 28-20 and, barring some sort of spectacular collapse in the final 18 minutes, through to the quarter-finals.

Clermont didn't just collapse, they imploded. The madness started when Julien Bardy was shown a yellow card for a dangerous tackle a minute after coming on as a sub. It was a stupid thing to do but I can't be too harsh on 'Bard'. Like me, he's always played the game right on the edge and sometimes you fall off that edge. Julien was singled out for criticism after the game but that was harsh. He's a hell of a good guy, a local lad who's worked really hard to get where he is today. His discipline has let him down at times but he's a player you'd always want playing for you and not against.

But Bard's yellow card was a lifeline for Bordeaux, who minutes before had appeared to be drowning under waves of Clermont's attack. Now the tide turned. First Paulin Riva scored a try, then Peter Saili went over, and with three minutes remaining Pierre Bernard kicked a penalty. In the space of ten minutes Clermont had gone from leading 28-20 to trailing 37-28. But there was still time.

The boys launched one final assault on the Bordeaux line and as the clocked ticked towards 80 minutes Clermont were awarded a penalty in front of the posts in the final minute. Kick it and we narrow the gap to six points, secure that precious losing point and go through to the last eight. I breathed a mighty sigh of relief. But Morgan tapped and went. Bordeaux defended their line and the window of opportunity slammed shut. Clermont were out of Europe and in the space of a couple of minutes we had become the laughing stock of Europe. It was unbelievable. Really. I could not believe what I had just seen.

Morgan took a heap of shit for his decision to tap and go, instead of taking the three points. That was unfair. He wasn't to blame. Jean-March Lhermet was.

Before the Bordeaux match Franck Azema had asked Jean-Marc to study every scenario possible that might arise during the game, and to also keep him abreast of what was happening in the other final group game between the Ospreys and Exeter. In other words it was Jean-Marc's job to give Franck and his coaching staff a running commentary on the state of the group with the results as they stood at any given moment in the two matches. Jean-Marc failed to do that. So no message was passed to Franck, and no message was passed to Morgan or the rest of the boys. It was utterly wrong for Morgan to take the shit for what happened. He had played 79 minutes of shattering rugby, he was fully focused on the moment, and it was up to the people with clearer heads to pass on the relevant information. Jean-Marc failed to do that, and frankly, I was surprised he still had a job the next day. His blunder must have cost Clermont about a million and a half euros in lost revenue. Even now I find it mind-boggling that Lhermet was so ridiculously inept.

I couldn't contain my anger and frustration. Picking up my phone I sent my now infamous tweet:

"Clean out The front office And #bringbackvern".

In hindsight it wasn't the best way to vent my frustration although the only regret I have is that Franck took it as a personal attack on him. It wasn't. The 'bringbackvern' hashtag was a moment of nostalgia on my part and it wasn't directed at Franck. The tweet was aimed at Lhermet, a culmination of all his incompetence over the years. On the Monday morning after the game the squad was called in so president Eric De Cromières could tear a strip of the players. As he did so Jean-Marc was standing next to the president staring the players down as if it was all our fault. Sure, the players deserved to take some shit - and they put their hands up and acknowledged their mistakes - but Lhermet definitely had a part to play in the shambles. Did he take his share of the blame? Hell, no.

In ice hockey terms, to 'clean out the front office' means to get rid of the general manager. That's what I wanted Clermont to do. And they did, six months later, finally sending Lhermet on his way.

But the immediate reaction from Clermont was to go after me. The tweet was nothing I hadn't said within the confines of the dressing room but the club had to be seen to punish me for fear of losing control of the squad completely. The day after the tweet De Cromières gave an interview in La Montagne in which he said I was out of order, adding that it was a "very stupid" act. That was fair enough but he then went too far, in my opinion, wondering if I was a little emotional internally because of my "little personal problems". Pretty cheap considering all my "little personal problems" were injuries sustained in the service of Clermont. But Eric was really getting his own back for the hornet's nest I had stirred up a few months earlier when my lawyer sent a letter to the club saying I wasn't happy with the way my concussion had been handled.

Some people asked why I didn't delete the tweet, as seems to be the fashion with any controversial statement put out on social media these days. In my opinion, deleting tweets makes the sender look weak. If you send it, stand by it. Sure, it's only 140 characters so it's a challenge to convey your message succinctly, but you can expand your point at a later date. But the bottom line is I didn't delete it because I stand by what I wrote.

The upshot was that I was fined a couple of grand for the tweet, and I had some work to do repairing my relationship with Franck. He and I have always been very honest with each other. He can be a hothead at times, such as when he went public with his criticisms of referee Alexandre Ruiz after Clermont's controversial loss to Racing 92 in last season's Top 14 semi-final. He went too far with what he said. Sure, be pissed off with the referee, but don't call him out in public.

But I've never had a problem with Franck. He's a good guy who's done well in filling the big shoes of Vern. Their approaches to coaching are fairly similar: an iron defence and an emphasis on doing the basics well so that the team is pulling in the same direction. Vern preferred a bit more volume and a bit more contact in training. We would go at almost full contact for four to five minutes with the ball in play non-stop. A decade ago that was innovative in the Top 14 and it put us head and shoulders above our Top 14 rivals between 2007 and 2010 in terms of fitness and execution. If I had one criticism of Vern in his last couple of seasons it would be that he could have given us more responsibility on the field, which is perhaps a strange criticism given that he's a Kiwi. If Vern was French it would be more understandable because French coaches don't like to give players much responsibility. They like to have total control. Again, it goes back to the importance in French society of hierarchy, having a clear chain of command, with people reluctant to delegate responsibility to subordinates for fear of being undermined.

I eventually made my return to the Clermont squad for the visit to Pau on May 7, coming off the bench for the last half an hour. It was good to be back, and good of Franck to bring me back into the fold. He could have treated me the same way that Jake White treated François Trinh-Duc in the same month. I thought that was disgusting of the Montpellier coach to deny such a great servant of the club a farewell appearance. White talked some bullshit about no place for sentiment, and, yes, it's now a professional sport but it still has some strong core values, without which it becomes just like any other business where ethics go out the window in the pursuit of profit. We can't let that happen to rugby.

Francois Trinh-Duc had spent 13 seasons at Montpellier, helped turn it from a small backwater club to the Top 14 finalists in 2011 and the European Challenge Cup winners in 2016. He, and the fans who loved him so much, deserved a chance to say their farewells, even if it was 15 minutes as a sub. It wasn't as if playing Trinh-Duc would have been a risk - he's won over 50 caps for France and is a very good player. In snubbing Trinh-Duc White came across as a small-minded and petty man, and I was surprised the club president, Mored Altrad, didn't intervene on Trinh-Duc's behalf.

Franck could have done something similar. I'd signed a deal with Oyonnax for the following season, I'd been out since Christmas and a lot of people would have understood if he didn't select me, particularly as I wasn't available for the play-offs because I was returning to Canada at the start of June to captain the side in our three summers Test matches.

But Franck's not a small-minded man, and a **fortnight after my comeback against Pau I was selected in the squad to play Stade Francais at the Stade Marcel-Michelin. It would be my last appearance in front of the Clermont fans and the end of an 11-year love affair.**

The week preceding the match was challenging. The hardest part was dealing with all the messages from well-wishers. They flooded in, from Canada, Wales and all over France. I always do my best to respond to messages so there was a lot of text messages flying back and forth that week. In addition we were in the process of selling our home, the house we'd built ourselves. That was an emotional wrench. So much of ourselves had been invested in the place that it felt like we were selling a bit of ourselves. To stand on the balcony and look out over the wonderful Auvergne countryside, Clermont visible in the distance, and know it was about to come to an end...it was tough. But part of my soul will always remain in the Auvergne, in this land of good, honest and above all loyal people.

I was named on the bench for the Stade match but Franck told me he bring me on with thirty minutes to go and he was true to his word. After 52 minutes of champing at the bit I was sent on

to replace Sébastien Vahaamahina. Never have I been so pumped up. In fact I was so pumped out I nearly took out Morgan Parra a couple of minutes later. I flew into the breakdown and caught the Little General with my shoulder. I think it was just as well he took the full brunt of my clearout because the referee asked to see the video replay to check I hadn't smashed a Stade player. They were nervous moments. I remember thinking, 'Oh no, not a yellow card in my final game'. Morgan sensed my apprehension because he made a joke out of it, telling the ref 'don't worry, he hit me. It's fine'. No action was taken and I repaid Morgan a couple of minutes later when I arrived at another breakdown. I thought about taking it on myself but then I glanced up, saw Mo had a metre of space out on the left, and popped a pass into his hands that enabled him to scamper over the try-line. But I couldn't let the Little General have the last word. That went to me, not with a try, but a whack on the head that saw me head off down the tunnel to be stitched. They must have been the quickest six stitches I've ever had. Three minutes later I was back, my head swathed in bandages, my beard dappled in blood. The fans roared. This was how they wanted to remember me.

The minutes after the final whistle were among the most memorable of my career. The boys' first reaction was to heave me onto their shoulders. That didn't last long. I could hear the gasps and groans above the noise of the crowd. Unbelievable, forced to do my lap of honour on my own two feet! It was an emotional experience. Pretty much the whole stadium had stayed behind and to hear nearly 20,000 people chant your name is an incredible sensation.

I got back into the corridor and then someone asked if I wanted to say a few words to the fans. Sure. It was all on the hoof and from the heart. I thanked the club and the players, but above all, the fans. The Yellow Army, the best supporters in the world. Truly formidable.

The celebrations continued long into the night, They began with a few beers in the changing room and then the squad had a dinner for wives and girlfriends. Finally a few of us retired to a secret little watering hole deep in the countryside. I'll say no more because some of those present had a match six days later.

Not me. On the Monday I went into the club to say goodbye to someone else who was leaving Clermont after years of long service. Mireille Charrier was retiring after many years as the club secretary. For the players she was the mother hen of the club, one of those people you find at all good rugby clubs around the world;

someone who does all the unglamorous but important behind the scenes work. In short, someone who makes sure everything works. I don't know which of us was the most emotional as we said our goodbyes.

Chapter Twenty One

It wasn't just a part of my soul I was leaving in Clermont, it was also a good row of vines! The Cudmore Sin Bin wine collection is the inspiration of my wife. Sustainability has always been very important to her, ever since her childhood in Newfoundland, where people relied on one another for survival during the long, brutal winters. You share everything, from fish to vegetables to meat and nothing went to waste. When Jennifer left Newfoundland and ventured out into the wider world she was overwhelmed to see all the waste that went on, particularly in Europe. So when it came to write her thesis for her MBA in 2010 - by now Jennifer was studying at Oxford - she combined her two passions, wine and sustainability, and produced a marketing report on sustainable luxury. Four years later the report formed the basis for the Sin Bin business plan.

In 2014 Maelle was was four and Grayson two so Jennifer had more time to herself and she wanted to get back in the workforce. The idea came to her while she was hiking in the hills around our home in Soulasse. Seeing all the vines, she suggested the idea of producing our own wine label playing in a tongue-in-cheek way on my rugby disciplinary record.

We dug out what she had written for her MBA and said 'yeah, let's turn this from just an idea into reality'. With our experience running the wine bar we had got to know quite a few people in the wine industry in the region and that was important:

we wanted to work with a local cave because Auvergne had been so good to us it would be a way of promoting the region while creating our own label. So we approached cave Saint-Verny, who are one of the sponsors of the club and they were huge on the idea, and thought it was fun and original.

With Saint-Vernay on board the next step was to approach a bank. That's where my reputation won the day. The business plan was OK but it had no detailed financial forecast. That didn't worry the bank. They loved the marketing concept of styling the Chardonny 'Yellow Card' and the Pinot Noir 'red card'.

It was a risk that could easily have backfired. But the secret behind the success of Sin Bin was that it didn't take itself seriously. If we had produced this rather pretentious label people would probably have muttered, 'who does Cudmore think he is, bringing out his own wine'? After all, Sebastian Chabel did that a few years ago, at the height of his fame, and it flopped. But we brought out a wine that laughed at my reputation, and people appreciated that, and laughed too. And of course it helps that it's a good wine.

We've since brought out a rosé and the latest label is 'Blood Brothers', a Bordeaux red that is a collaboration with Damien Chouly and Nick Abendanon. Again that was Jennifer's idea. She wanted a wine that would capture rugby's 'band of brothers'' camaraderie and over several enjoyable dinners with Damien and Nick we came up with Blood Brothers. Nick's dad is a connoisseur and he contacted a château in Bordeaux and made things happen.

Having the wine business based in Clermont gives me the chance to return regularly to the town to catch up with friends but I've no regrets about leaving the club. My time was up at Clermont. For a start they've got three fine young second-rows in Arthur Iturria, Paul Jedrasiak and Sébastien Vahaamahina but above all my relationship with Jean-Marc Lhermet and Eric de Cromières was beyond repair because of the fall-out from the way my concussion was treated.

I was mad as hell, to be honest, but I challenged that anger in a positive way, establishing the Rugby Safety Network. Jennifer was instrumental in its foundation because she suffered just as me from what I went through in the summer of 2015.

Sure, I was the one lying one the couch with the physical pain but my wife had to bear the emotional pain, and she doesn't want other partners of rugby players to endure what she did.

The two tenets of the Rugby Safety Network are 'support' and 'education': support for players - and their families - who suffer concussion, and education for everyone involved in the sport so that we find ways to better protect players.

Every concussion case is different and must be treated on a case by case basis. In the past the attitude was, at best, slapdash, and at worst downright negligent. That has to stop because I still don't think World Rugby quite realises that they are sitting on a timebomb. Look at the United States, where in 2015 a federal judge found in favour of a class-action lawsuit brought by more than 20,000 retired players against the National Football League [NFL]. That agreement will provide as much as $5 million per retired player for serious medical conditions brought on by repeated head trauma, so it's estimated that the NFL will pay out $765 million in compensation to former players in the years ahead.

Not surprisingly that has sent a shiver through World Rugby particularly given the number of players who are being forced into premature retirement by concussion issues. At the start of the 2015-16 season, for example, Ireland prop Nathan White, Saracens second-row Alistair Hargreaves and Connacht centre Dave McSharry - who was just 26 - all retired because of head trauma. I've nothing but the highest regard for them because to walk away from the sport you love, the sport that has been your life for years, and that's become like an extended family, is traumatic. But ultimately rugby is only a game and it's not worth jeopardizing your health in the long-term just for another season or two's rugby.

But there are plenty of other players who are still playing and still carrying the effects of past concussions. When I went to La Nuit du Rugby award ceremony in Paris in October 2016 I talked to a lot of players from Top 14 and ProD2 clubs about concussion, and what I heard disturbed me. These were stories of guys who, having been concussed, were put back on the field after just a week's rest because they did OK in the six-day protocol. This protocol is supposed to determine whether a player, over the course of six days, has sufficiently recovered to start training again. But the problem with the six-day protocol is that it leaves the player susceptible to second impact problems, and that's what really laid me low in 2015.

We're making slow progress, and in France, at least, Clermont are taking the initiative. It was good to see in October that both Damien Chouly and Fritz Lee were rested for an important European tie against Bordeaux because of blows to the head sustained the previous week. In the past the club might have been tempted to play one of them - as they're both back-row players - but in this instance they put player welfare above results. Long may it continue.

Clermont are also at the forefront in France of using blood protein levels to determine the extent of a player's head trauma. This is the protein S-100B which, if tests show a high level, can indicate the presence of neuropathological conditions such as concussion. However, I have a degree of scepticism about these tests because some people have naturally higher levels of the protein than others. So while it's a guideline it's not foolproof.

 It's why as I said the guiding principle of the Rugby Safety Network is education. The reason why I've been able to continue playing is because of the education I've received in concussion. I've had the good fortune to work with some fine doctors in Canada and more recently with Neurovision Consulting in Geneva, who are now one of the Rugby Safety Network's partners. Their specialists have worked with Formula One drivers, NASA and the European Space Commission, and the baseline Tests they've produced for rugby are the way forward. They examine the brain through the eyes, looking at how the eyes follow light, how they react to it, their converge. The eyes are the window into the brain and will reveal more about a player's head trauma than a blood protein test.

What I find mystifying is that these baseline tests - that I first did playing club rugby in Canada fifteen years ago - have not been introduced into professional French rugby, which is indicative of the time lag that exists between France and the English-speaking world when it comes to sports science.

There's no doubt that the UK is ahead of France in dealing with concussion:

perhaps it's because of the common language and the fact it's easier for them to learn from North America, who are leading the way in addressing the issue, not just the NFL but also in Canada. I was heartened in the summer of 2016 to see that the Ontario legislature passed Rowan's Law, named in memory of Rowan Stringer, a 17-year-old Ottawa girl who died in 2013 after suffering two concussions in one week while playing high school rugby. The aim of Ronan's Law is to educate coaches in the prevention and diagnosis of head injuries and then manage their return to playing. I hope the law is rolled out across the rest of Canada because then people will be obliged to follow the guidelines otherwise they'll be breaking the law.

It's not as if France doesn't have specialists in the field of neurosurgery. Dr Francois Chermann is one of best neurologists around, and he's done some work with the LNR in the past but his experience and expertise isn't being utilised the way it should. Which is another reason why we are determined to spread the message of our Rugby Safety Network across France.

Let me give you an example. At the start of this season a young Canadian kid playing at a Top 14 club had a pretty bad concussion and was sent to see the neurologist on the Monday. "Come back in 15 days but in the meantime don't do any training, don't drive, avoid bright lights and stay away from computers and ipads", he was told. All good advice. The next day the player turned up at his club to tell them what the neurologist said, and the team doctor told him to get on the bike and start the six-day protocol. So he did, because he was a young kid who felt under pressure and feared for his place in the squad. Needless to say he started having headaches and feeling unwell. Fortunately had the strength of character to get off the back and defy the team doctor.

In contrast look at the far more rigorous approach to head injuries in England. At the start of the 2016-17 season, the Aviva Premiership became the first domestic league to trial real-time pitchside concussion video reviews. These were successfully used during the 2015 World Cup, and the English clubs were so impressed that, with support from the Rugby Football Union, they implemented the technology last year. In my view it's one of the most important innovations the sport has witnessed in the professional era. Each of the 12 Premiership clubs has a Pitchside Video Reviewer (PVR), who is trained member of their medical staff, watching the match on an iPad. If a player takes a blow to the head then these PVRs are able to analyse the injury within seconds. If they believe the player requires a Head Injury Assessment (HIA) they will tell the team doctor and the referee will send the player off for a check-up.

These pitchside iPads were used in last season's Top 14 play-offs but they weren't retained for the 2015-16 regular season. Why not? They are a crucial tool in the concussion campaign but it encapsulates the misguided and misinformed approach of French rugby to the issue. French clubs like to boast about how good they are with the treatment of players once they've been concussed, but the problem in the Top 14 is their Heat-of-the-Moment care. Players who are concussed during a match still aren't being withdrawn immediately because the tools aren't in place to identity the concussion, and clubs are reluctant to stand down players for big matches.

I give you as an example Liam Gill and Charles Ollivon, the Toulon back-row forwards, who were both concussed against Clermont in September. Watch the footage. The pair dropped like stones - in separate incidents - after head knocks, and Ollivon appeared to be unconscious. Both were taken off, and yet both played seven days later against Montpellier.

As I've said, clubs don't send a player out to play if he's got a damaged hamstring so why do it with a damaged head? It's crazy.

*

'Crazy' is also a word one could you to describe the global rugby calendar, and having endured it for fifteen years perhaps I'm in a position to pass one or two comments. This season at Oyonnax has been my first as a professional player without playing in a European competition, and it makes a huge difference because you don't feel you're on an endless treadmill of high-pressure rugby.

There were times during my eleven years at Clermont when one match just merged into another and it felt like a war of attrition and not a game of rugby. The toughest time was December and January when there are four rounds of the Champions Cup and a string of big Top 14 matches. The weather is grim - bitterly cold and sometimes snowing - and the rugby is often just as unpleasant. I don't know what it's like for spectators but for players it's not much fun playing rugby in the depth of the northern hemisphere winter. The warm months of May and June feel a hell of a long way-off and I'd be lying if I said it didn't at times feel like a slog.

It must feel even worse for the players who emerge from those two months and then go straight into the Six Nations. At least the rest of us could get a couple of weeks' rest. Frankly, I don't know how the French internationals cope. Their clubs treat them like horses, working them until they don't win anymore and then throwing them out, while the media and the public expect them to perform miracles on the pitch. It's a miracle that they're still standing by February, so don't expect them to suddenly roll back the years and play with that famous 'French flair'. Those days are gone, and they're never coming back. I think the France national team will continue to decline because the clubs have so much power and they're not interested in the fortunes of the national side.

I would like to see a winter break introduced into French rugby, and indeed all European rugby, similar to what the Bundesliga, the German football league, does every winter when it shuts down from mid December to mid January. A month for the players to rest and recuperate, head to warmer climes for a week and let their bodies knit back together.

Will it ever happen? What do you think? The powers-that-be are interested in profit, not players, and I can never see a day when the Top 14 will take a month off. So we'll continue as we are, flogging ourselves week after week - for 44 weeks of the year - and the quality of rugby will continue to deteriorate because everyone is so exhausted.

I read last year that a handful of Top 14 presidents were in favour of expanding the league to sixteen clubs, which I found utterly ridiculous. That would mean more matches and also a couple of more clubs who aren't of the required standard to be competitive in the top flight. We see it every season in the Top 14, a couple of clubs who struggle from the start and end up becoming the whipping boys. That's why I'm in favour of reducing the Top 14 by two: it would mean fewer matches but make them more competitive. I'd keep promotion and relegation, though just the one club, because you've got to hold out hope to clubs that they can join the big boys. And the public likes a rag to riches story, whether it's what Max Guazzini did with Stade Francais twenty years ago or what Oyonnax achieved in climbing into the Top 14 in 2013.

But that's for the suits to decide, and I can safely say I'll never cross to the dark side and become a fully paid-up member of the Rugby Establishment! I'd never pass the entrance exam.

Obviously I want to stay involved in the game when I retire, whenever that may be. I've been doing quite a bit of coaching this season at Oyonnax - out of necessity, admittedly, having broken my hand in the first league game of the season - but if you're going to be sidelined for a couple of months, throwing yourself into coaching is a pretty good way of burning off the frustration. I really enjoy it, whether it's with the youth team or the senior players, and I was fortunate last year to spend a few weeks working with the Canada national squad. 'Giving something back to the game' may be a cliche but it's how most players feel about the sport we love so much.

And I guess in my case it rings particularly true. I started this book by recounting the day I walked out of prison nearly twenty years ago, the first steps on an extraordinary journey on which during the last eleven years I have been accompanied by my beautiful wife.

Behind me every step of the way have been my mum and dad. When I look back on my troubled youth it's not with any sense of shame. I didn't go around terrorising people intentionally but there's no doubt my rambunctious behaviour upset quite a few people. But it did more than that to my parents. It caused them a great deal of distress and that I regret.

I'll end with a story. One day when I was Fraser Regional Correction Centre Concorde flew past en route to Vancouver airport. I heard it before I saw it, so I rushed to the window of my cell and watched in awe as it passed overhead. It was a beautiful sight and it left me transfixed for the rest of the day.

But it was more than just its beauty. It's what that Concorde represented, a triumph for endeavour over scepticism and for belief over doubt. People had said it would never get off the ground, but it did, and when I left prison some people said I would never go straight, but I did.

Thanks to rugby.

[ends]

Appendix:

From Capilano to Canada to Clermont, I've been fortunate to play with some of the great players of their generation. Some are world-famous, others less so, but there are the fifteen players I'd select in my All-time XV.

15: Nick Abendanon: One of the best-counter attackers I've seen, Nick has the flair that the French used to have. Great twinkle toes and he knows a lot about wine.

14: Napolioni Nalaga: A force of nature, Naps has hands the size of dinner plates and spends a lot of the time giggling. Burst onto the scene in 2007 for Clermont & spent the next seven years scoring crazy tries.

13: Nick Blevins: As a kid Nick wanted to play football in the NFL. That didn't work out and 'Smoky' switched to rugby and it's been a pleasure playing with Nick in the last two World Cups

12: Bob Bremner: Played with Bob for the Capilanos back in the day. A mountain of a man who was always fired up to play and had a ferocious will to win.

11: DTH van der Merwe: He's a South Africa through and through but he converted to the Canadian spirit after his family emigrated. A huge asset to Canadian rugby with 20 tries in 35 Tests.

10: Nick Belmar: I've known many good fly-halves but Nick played ten when I was at Capilanos, and he was Mr Reliable. Nick could have played representative rugby but he was one of those guys who loved playing all sports.

9: Morgan Parra: There were times when I could happily have smacked the Little General! Gee, he can be a pain in the ass. But Morgan is a hell of a competitor and as brave as they come.

8: Damien Chouly: My old mate, Damien, not only a friend but a world-class player. Always puts in a good shift, never shirks his responsibility, and one of the few guys I've never seen have a really bad game. He's also a pretty decent D.J.

7: Julien Bardy: Tough choice between Alexandre Audebert & Bard, but I've gone for Julien. Got a lot of time for him. Like me he plays on the edge, and like me he sometimes goes over it, but he's a dog at the breakdown.

6: Sam Broomhall: Played with Sam in my early days at Clermont and one of the most naturally gifted players I've ever seen. Always did the right thing at the right time on the field and never made a wrong decision.

5: Thibaut Privat: We never had huge conversations but we've always understood each other. Shared many hard moments together, and that's created a mutual respect that will last forever.

4: Jamie Cudmore: I've picked myself, just ahead of Nathan Hines. It's my book!

3: Martin Scelzo: Only ever one choice - Martin 'Man and a half' Scelzo. The guy is huge, a refrigerator on legs. Locking the scrum behind him was great. I could roll a smoke and enjoy the ride. Also very entertaining off the field with his singing, dancing and stories about Maradona.

2: Benjamin Kayser: Mario Ledesma was an outstanding hooker but I've gone for Ben. Similar in style to Mario and just as intelligent, Ben gets the nod because he speaks four languages and can sweet-talk the refs.

1: Hubert Buydens: We call him 'cowhead' and he's the hairiest man in world rugby, but I've played Test match rugby with Hubert for ten years and he's an awesome scrummager.

Manufactured by Amazon.ca
Bolton, ON

10807169R00106